D0783764

Electronic Resources in the Virtual Learning Environment

CHANDOS
INFORMATION PROFESSIONAL SERIES

Series Editor: Ruth Rikowski
(email: rikowski@tiscali.co.uk)

Chandos' new series of books are aimed at the busy information professional. They have been specially commissioned to provide the reader with an authoritative view of current thinking. They are designed to provide easy-to-read and (most importantly) practical coverage of topics that are of interest to librarians and other information professionals. If you would like a full listing of current and forthcoming titles, please visit our website **www.chandospublishing.com** or contact Hannah Grace-Williams on email info@chandospublishing.com or telephone number +44 (0) 1865 884447.

New authors: we are always pleased to receive ideas for new titles; if you would like to write a book for Chandos, please contact Dr Glyn Jones on email gjones@chandospublishing.com or telephone number +44 (0) 1865 884447.

Bulk orders: some organisations buy a number of copies of our books. If you are interested in doing this, we would be pleased to discuss a discount. Please contact Hannah Grace-Williams on email info@chandospublishing.com or telephone number +44 (0) 1865 884447.

Electronic Resources in the Virtual Learning Environment

A guide for librarians

JANE SECKER

Chandos Publishing

Oxford · England · New Hampshire · USA

Chandos Publishing (Oxford) Limited
Chandos House
5 & 6 Steadys Lane
Stanton Harcourt
Oxford OX29 1RL
UK
Tel: +44 (0) 1865 884447 Fax: +44 (0) 1865 884448
Email: info@chandospublishing.com
www.chandospublishing.com

Chandos Publishing USA
3 Front Street, Suite 331
PO Box 338
Rollinsford, NH 03869
USA
Tel: 603 749 9171 Fax: 603 749 6155
Email: BizBks@aol.com

First published in Great Britain in 2004

ISBN:
1 84334 059 3 (paperback)
1 84334 060 7 (hardback)

© J. Secker, 2004

British Library Cataloguing-in-Publication Data.
A catalogue record for this book is available from the British Library.

All rights reserved. No part of this publication may be reproduced, stored in or introduced into
a retrieval system, or transmitted, in any form, or by any means (electronic, mechanical,
photocopying, recording or otherwise) without the prior written permission of the Publishers.
This publication may not be lent, resold, hired out or otherwise disposed of by way of trade in
any form of binding or cover other than that in which it is published without the prior consent
of the Publishers. Any person who does any unauthorised act in relation to this publication may
be liable to criminal prosecution and civil claims for damages.

The Publishers make no representation, express or implied, with regard to the accuracy of the
information contained in this publication and cannot accept any legal responsibility or liability
for any errors or omissions.

The material contained in this publication constitutes general guidelines only and does not
represent to be advice on any particular matter. No reader or purchaser should act on the basis
of material contained in this publication without first taking professional advice appropriate to
their particular circumstances.

Cover images courtesy of Bytec Solutions Ltd (*www.bytecweb.com*) and David Hibberd
(*DAHibberd@aol.com*).

Typeset by Concerto, Leighton Buzzard, Bedfordshire, UK (01525 378757)
Printed in the UK and USA

Contents

Introduction

The education sector today is undergoing fundamental changes, driven partly by advances in information and communication technologies (ICTs). No one working in this sector today can ignore the increasing emphasis of e-learning on teaching and research programmes. In the UK, the importance of e-learning has been recognised by the Department for Education and Skills (DfES) which published a consultation document in 2003 to formulate an 'e-learning strategy' for the entire education sector (DfES, 2003: see Chapter 2). Libraries have traditionally held an important role in the learning and teaching activities of universities: students had to come into the library to find books and journals. However, with an increasing amount of electronic resources available outside the library, from the desktop, it is easy to see how both the learner and the teacher might bypass the library altogether. Many early initiatives in e-learning in higher education have been led by technologists, educators and administrators and only in a few instances were such initiatives led by librarians. In many organisations, librarians have had to fight for recognition and demonstrate how they can add value to the e-learning process. Yet, research programmes, funded by the Joint Information Systems Committee (JISC) in the UK and the National Science Foundation (NSF) in the US, provide evidence to demonstrate the valuable contribution librarians can make. There are obvious benefits to integrated learning systems; meanwhile, collaboration between the e-learning and library communities is also crucial.

I wrote this book partly in recognition that I am a librarian in a fortunate position within my organisation. Not only has the London School of Economics and Political Science recognised for many years that e-learning and libraries are connected, but I work in a team alongside technologists and educators. As e-learning initiatives are set up in my institution, teachers are reminded of the relevance of library resources. However, I recognise that many librarians do not work in such an environment. Therefore, for them it is even more important to read this book, to understand how they can contribute to e-learning and then to take action. This book is in part a call to librarians, across the education sector to open up a dialogue with educators and technologists to ensure that the e-learning revolution does not leave the profession standing on the sidelines with others questioning our relevance.

This book is particularly aimed at librarians and other information professionals working in the education sector, although I hope that librarians in other sectors may find it useful. It provides an overview of recent developments in both the library world and the wider education sector. The book charts the recent development of both digital libraries and virtual learning environments and shows how these systems are increasingly being integrated to improve the learning experience. Wherever possible, examples of both research and practice are provided. As e-learning proliferates across the sectors to businesses, government departments, schools and colleges, this book should be relevant to information professionals in these fields as well.

Both the digital library and e-learning fields have seen rapid developments in recent years. Therefore to provide a context, the book examines key developments throughout the 1990s, when many pioneering initiatives took place. Some of the work of the UK Electronic Libraries (eLib) Programme, funded by JISC, is particularly relevant to this book and initiatives such as the Teaching and Learning Technologies Programme (TLTP) funded by the Higher Education Funding Council for England (HEFCE) are also examined. The first two chapters describe research and developments in two fields, which in many ways occurred in parallel to each other. However, in 2001, the launch of the Digital Libraries and Virtual Learning Environments (DiVLE) programme signified the integration of two previously separate initiatives, and has led to the establishment of important links between the two communities. The programme was important in bringing together communities of professionals, in the form of learning or educational· technologists and librarians. It also led to many commercial partnerships between library software vendors and the e-learning industry. Elsewhere, joint initiatives between JISC and the NSF also brought together the e-learning and library communities.

This book recognises that the information environment is changing enormously and that the learning solutions are becoming increasingly digital. Therefore new approaches and practical solutions for librarians are vital if the profession is to remain relevant and focused on the needs of users.

Structure of the book

Chapter 1 provides a context to the book, exploring the development of the digital library since the 1990s. It includes an up-to-date definition of the term today, but explains the background to this development, including the importance of the Follett Report in the UK in 1993 which led to the launch of the eLib Programme. The chapter also describes how electronic resources have proliferated since this time, and describes the changing information environment where e-journals and e-books are increasingly the norm.

Chapter 2 briefly describes the development of e-learning, focusing on higher education in the UK. Starting with the Dearing Report in 1997 it traces the development through to 2003, when the Department for Education and Skills published its 'e-learning strategy' as a discussion paper. Again the Funding Councils have been instrumental in bringing about change in this area, with approaches such as the Teaching and Learning Technology Programme (TLTP) supporting initiatives across the UK. The situation in both the UK and US is compared, but the movements towards flexible learning and distance learning is outlined. This chapter also focuses on the commercial vendors who have capitalised on developments in this area and developed products such as virtual learning environments (VLEs). Finally, the chapter provides an overview of the JISC DiVLE Programme, which was so timely in the writing of this book.

Chapter 3 looks specifically at information literacy and its relevance to e-learning. It highlights how the role of the information professional has shifted towards an increased emphasis on the librarian as an educator in his or her own right. It considers the skills required to be an information professional today. The chapter argues that a sound information literacy strategy is crucial to combat the 'Google generation' and the chapter looks at the librarian's role in the growing team of learning support staff.

Chapter 4 considers issues of copyright and licensing, which are becoming increasingly important in the digital environment. The chapter provides an overview of copyright law relating to educational institutions in the UK, US and Australia. It also considers various licensing schemes issued by reprographic rights organisations. Finally, the chapter recognises that librarians have a new important advisory role when staff want to use resources in e-learning. They should capitalise on this expertise to encourage appropriate and fair use of resources.

Chapter 5 looks at technical issues associated with e-learning and digital libraries. It is particularly concerned with standards and specifications in both fields. It also considers issues of access and authentication to ensure the appropriate use of resources. E-learning standards and specifications are considered. The chapter also provides a brief overview of metadata, library resources and learning objects.

Finally, to illustrate many of the ideas discussed in earlier chapters, Chapter 6 provides a series of case studies from universities in the UK. These illustrate ways in which librarians have become involved in e-learning initiatives or ways in which library systems can become more integrated with e-learning. The final example in the book is a guide to linking electronic journal resources.

Definitions

It is important that readers understand the terminology used in this book and the definition of key terms. In writing this book it became clear that language and terminology presented something of a problem. Initially there are problems working in a cross-disciplinary area and generally librarians and learning technologists have quite separate and distinct cultures and languages. Among librarians from the UK and US there is generally a consensus about the key terminology used and there are few problems with the term 'digital library', which is used throughout. Its use is widespread in the US and although 'electronic library' is often used in the UK, digital library is becoming increasingly common. However, terms that emerge from the learning technology field are more problematic, including the term 'learning technology' itself, which, while prevalent in the UK and Australia, is substituted for the term 'educational technology' in the US. Similarly the term 'virtual learning environment' is widespread throughout the UK, but such a package is generally defined as a learning management system (LMS) in the US. This abbreviation brings additional confusion to UK librarians as LMS is commonly known as the library management system. In an attempt to resolve these problems each chapter defines the key terms used.

Finally, in writing a book about an aspect of technology, the reader should be aware that change can often be fast-paced. Therefore it is anticipated that specific tools and technologies referred to throughout the book will evolve and develop over time. It is important for librarians to recognise that e-learning is a topic that they will need to remain engaged with, and that journals and other professional literature are vital sources for up-to-date information to supplement this book.

Acknowledgements

I should like to thank the following people for their advice, help and support while writing this book: Lyn Parker and Peter Stubley from the University of Sheffield; Debbi Boden and Sue Holloway from Imperial College, London; the LSE Centre for Learning Technology, in particular, Steve Ryan. Thanks also to Maria Bell, Grazia Manzotti and Gwyneth Price. Finally, special thanks to Tim for his encouragement and support.

I am grateful to Toby Bainton from SCONUL for permission to reproduce the diagram on page 60, and to Bob Powell and the British Educational Communications and Technology Agency (Becta) for permission to reproduce their diagram on page 37. I am also grateful to Imperial College for permission to reproduce the screenshots in Case study 4 (Chapter 6).

About the author

Jane Secker is currently employed as the Learning Technology Librarian at the London School of Economics and Political Science (LSE). She works in the Centre for Learning Technology supporting and advising academic staff. Prior to this she was employed as Project Officer at University College, London and at the Library of the Natural History Museum. She was recently seconded to work on the JISC-funded DELIVER Project undertaking the user needs analysis.

Jane is the Chair of the HERON User Group, which represents over 70 HERON members. She is also the Chair of ASSIGN (Aslib Social Science Information Group and Network) and a member of Aslib Council. She serves on the editorial board of *Program*.

Jane has a PhD and first degree from the University of Wales, Aberystwyth. Her research was a study of newspaper collections in libraries and their value to historians. It focused on issues such as the preservation and digitisation of newspaper collections.

The author can be contacted at the following address:

Dr Jane Secker
Learning Technology Librarian
Centre for Learning Technology
LSE
Houghton Street
London
WC2A 2AE

E-mail: *j.secker@lse.ac.uk*

The digital library

Introduction

This chapter outlines the development of the digital library in its current form, thereby providing a context for the integration of library resources with virtual or e-learning environments. Many services and systems which make up the digital library have been developed during the past decade. This chapter examines the concept of the digital library, providing a definition for the reader. To place the book within a wider context, the chapter then goes on to discuss some key digital library research, concentrating on developments in the UK and the US. In the UK, research has been largely funded by the Joint Information Systems Committee (JISC) Electronic Libraries Programme (eLib). In the US, digital library projects have been funded throughout the 1990s by the National Science Foundation (NSF). Most recently these developments have come together with the joint JISC–NSF programme, 'Digital Libraries in the Classroom' which is discussed in more detail in Chapter 2.

The chapter does not set out to provide a comprehensive overview of all digital library developments. It is not possible in one chapter to discuss such developments comprehensively and there are other books available which do this in some detail. For example, Lesk (1997) provides an overview of digital library developments, whereas Borgman (2003) examines what is called the global information infrastructure (GII). However, the chapter does discuss research and developments in the past decade that have shaped today's information environment. The second half of the chapter includes a description of some of the key components, and the respective systems that make up the digital library today. Until recently the term digital library was often taken to mean an online catalogue or library management system. However, this now encompasses a range of tools to manage electronic books, e-journals, digital rights and the wealth of electronic resources.

Defining the digital library

Since the 1970s developments in computer technology have impacted upon all areas of human activity. These changes have led to the concept of the information society, which has been defined as:

> A society in which the quality of life, as well as prospects for social change and economic development, depend increasingly upon information and its exploitation. (Martin, 1995, p. 3)

Although the reality of this information society is still being debated, developments in information and communications technologies (ICTs) are central to this book. The Internet has provided a global communication network and increasingly the importance of digital information is recognised. Concepts such as the 'global village' and 'digital revolution' are referred to with increasing frequency by authors. In *The Rise of the Network Society*, Castells (1996) provides a contemporary account of the economic and social dynamics of the new age of information. He formulated a systematic theory of the information society, which took account of the fundamental effects of information technology on contemporary society.

ICTs have had an effect on all aspects of the library profession. The phrase 'digital library' is used with increasing frequency and it has been defined as:

> ... the widely accepted term describing the use of digital technologies to acquire, store, preserve and provide access to information and material originally published in digital form or digitised from existing print, audio-visual and other forms. (Lang, 1998, p. 227)

Meanwhile, DELOS (2001) argued that digital libraries should:

> ... enable any citizen to access all human knowledge any time and anywhere, in a friendly, multi-modal, efficient, and effective way, by overcoming barriers of distance, language, and culture and by using multiple Internet-connected devices.

Crawford and Gorman (1995, pp. 123–30) have questioned the wisdom of this increasing emphasis on digital information when considering the future role of libraries. While remaining advocates of technology, the authors recognise that the library profession and the wider world should not assume that digital means better and:

Libraries will and should continue to use a mix of book and other linear document collections, paper journal subscriptions, electronic network-based distribution, full-text CD-ROM, CD-ROM indexes with full-text microfiche, tape-loaded databases, Eureka and CitaDel, EPIC, FirstSearch and OCLC delivery services, UnCover, Dialog, Nexis and others. (Crawford and Gorman, 1995, p. 176)

In the 1990s, developments in the UK were funded under a programme of research called the Electronic Libraries Programme (eLib) which is discussed later in this chapter. This led the UK to adopt the term 'electronic library' which still persists in many institutions. UK-funded research helped coin the term 'hybrid library' and Rusbridge (1998) has argued that the concept of the 'hybrid library' was a logical follow-on from current developments. As digital library activities continued within institutions, Rusbridge argued that users required the sort of integration of digital library services which the hybrid library promised. However, increasingly, in both the UK and US as well as elsewhere in the world, the term digital library is generally understood and has an agreed definition.

Global digital library initiatives

A number of large libraries throughout the world became involved in digital library initiatives in the early 1990s, with much pioneering work being undertaken in the US. In 1992 Cornell University formed the Digital Access Coalition to explore the use of digital imagery. This group has now been superseded by the Cornell Institute for Digital Collections (CIDC) which has made numerous resources available in electronic format.[1] Similarly, Project Open Book at Yale University was another early initiative in digital collections. Launched in 1992, this project sought to convert 10,000 microfilmed volumes of nineteenth- and twentieth-century books into digital format. Through the Electronic Text Center members of the university can now gain access to digitised original material.[2] The US Digital Libraries Initiative (DLI), funded by the National Science Foundation (NSF) and launched in 1994, sought to 'dramatically advance the means to collect, store, and organize information in digital forms, and make it available for searching, retrieval, and processing via communication networks'.[3] Rusbridge (1998) defined the DLI as 'research' rather than development and although the 'results are exciting and extraordinarily interesting, ... it is very hard to determine how many of these ideas might be effectively deployed in real life situations.' The DLI Phase 1 ran from 1994 until 1998; many of the Phase 2 projects started in 1999 and a number are still funded until August 2004 or 2005. The projects are based at major US universities with a team of investigators. Many are concerned with developing a digital library of specific resources, for example the National Gallery of the Spoken Word based at Michigan State University (more information at *http://www.ngsw.org/*) or PERSIVAL (PErsonalized Retrieval and Summarization of Image, Video and Language Resource: *http://persival.cs.columbia.edu/*) which is a project based at Columbia University for building a Digital Library for Patient Care.

The international digital libraries programme

In 1998 the NSF issued a call for proposals to begin addressing some of the research challenges associated with creating international digital libraries. The call requested multi-country, multi-team projects involving at least one research team in the United States and one in another country. The NSF would support the US part of a joint project while the non-US parts needed to gain their support from other sources. The UK Joint Information Systems Committee (JISC) was the first to join the NSF in this endeavour and issued a matching call. JISC committed £500,000 per year for three years to fund new development work in this programme. The NSF committed a similar amount. The German Research Foundation, the Deutsche Forschungsgemeinschaft (DSF) and the European Union also joined the NSF to work on collaborative digital library projects.

The programme aimed to create innovative and beneficial ways to access networked resources. It planned to make many software tools available for wider use. Specific objectives of the programme were to:

- assemble collections of information that are not otherwise accessible or usable because of technical barriers, distance, size, system fragmentation or other limits;
- create new technology and the understanding to make it possible for a distributed set of users to find, deliver and exploit such information;
- evaluate the effect of this new technology and its international benefits.[4]

This programme ran from August 1999 until July 2003. Projects investigated topics such as using the Open Archives Initiative (OAI) to set up an e-print archive (discussed in more detail in Chapter 5), digital preservation, cross-domain searching and metadata construction. They included projects such as:

- Open Citation Project: looking at the set up of e-print archives: *http://opcit.eprints.org/*
- Cross-domain Resource Discovery: *http://sca.lib.liv.ac.uk/cheshire/*
- HARMONY: metadata for resource discovery of multimedia digital objects: *http://www.ilrt.bris.ac.uk/discovery/harmony/*
- IMESH Toolkit: an architecture and toolkit for distributed subject gateways: *http://www.ukoln.ac.uk/metadata/imesh-toolkit/*
- Online Music Recognition and Searching: *http://www.omras.org/*

These projects raised many issues which remain topical for digital libraries, including the setting up of e-print archives, metadata construction and cross-domain searching. Of these projects, the Open Citation Project is discussed in more detail later in this chapter.

Much of the pioneering digital library research concentrated on the technicalities of the digitisation process. Scanning material to create images was relatively unproblematic, although the real benefit of digitisation comes from facilitating access to the text of material. Many experiments to perfect techniques such as optical character recognition (OCR), used to convert scanned images into machine-readable text, were undertaken, and a large amount of literature was generated for librarians, such as that by Ogg (1992). Later digital library projects were more concerned with issues such as sustainability and interoperability. These issues, among others, were identified by DELOS (2001) in their paper 'Digital Libraries: Future Directions for a European Research Programme' which set out a framework for research for the European Union from 2002 to 2006.

UK digital library initiatives

In the UK during the corresponding period, the British Library was one of the key players in developments and initiatives in digitisation. The British Library's Strategic Objectives, published in 1993, stated that by the year 2000 it would be a major centre for the storage of, and access to, digital texts. This led to the launch of the Initiatives for Access programme, a series of projects and experiments using ICTs to facilitate access to collections. For example, one of the first projects resulted in the production of a digital version of the *Beowulf* manuscript, now available on the British Library's website. The programme was regarded as an overwhelming success and is documented in the 1998 publication *Towards a Digital Library* (Carpenter et al., 1998). In developing the digital library, the British Library sought to improve access, for all users, to their collections. The Library also hoped digitisation would have benefits for the conservation and preservation of collections, in particular those which are fragile, of high value or heavily used.

Increasingly in the late 1990s, public libraries in Britain were becoming important providers of electronic information, as recognised by the publication of *New Library: The People's Network* (LIC, 1997). Commissioned by the Department for Culture, Media and Sport, and undertaken by the Library and Information Commission (LIC), the report concluded that although printed publications will remain important, the role of public libraries in providing access to, and delivery of, electronic information is expected to increase, particularly for educational and reference works and government and local information. *New Library* proposed the creation of a UK Public Library Network, connecting every public library to the Internet. Public libraries are also central to government moves towards the concept of 'lifelong learning' and the National Grid for Learning. Furthermore, they have been recognised as fulfilling an important function as repositories for community history.

The role of JISC

The Joint Information Systems Committee (JISC) has arguably had by far the greatest impact on the development of the digital library. JISC is funded by the UK's Further and Higher Education Funding Councils for England, Scotland and Wales. Established in 1993, the Committee was set up to deal with networking and specialist information services. Its remit is to work with further and higher education to provide strategic guidance, advice and opportunities to use ICT to support teaching, learning, research and administration. JISC operates through a committee system whose members are made up of senior managers, academics and technology experts working in UK further and higher education. An executive in turn supports these committees, which formulate policy and manage the JISC-funded services and strategic development programmes. JISC provides a centralised and coordinated direction for the development of the infrastructure and activities, in line with its five-year strategy. Specifically it provides:

- new environments for learning, teaching and research;
- access to electronic resources;
- a world-class network – JANET (Joint Academic NETwork);
- guidance on institutional change;
- advisory and consultancy services;
- regional support centres (RSCs) for further education colleges.

An important part of the role of JISC has been funding for projects in all areas of information and communication technologies. For libraries, however, the most important programme was the Electronic Libraries Programme (eLib).

The Electronic Libraries Programme (eLib)

The Electronic Libraries Programme (eLib) was launched in 1994 by the JISC as a direct response to the 1993 Libraries Review by the UK Higher Education Funding Councils, known as the Follett Report (HEFCE, 1993). Much of this work was pioneering and laid the foundations of the digital library as we know it today. The entire programme was divided into three phases, the first two having a budget of £15 million over three years to fund projects in a variety of areas. The main aim of the eLib programme, through its projects, was to engage the higher education community in developing and shaping the implementation of the electronic library. In Phases 1 and 2, projects were funded in areas such as on-demand publishing, electronic document delivery, electronic journals, images and digitisation. Phase 3 of eLib was again a three-year programme with a budget of £4.1 million. Launched in 1997 research into areas such as hybrid libraries, preservation and projects into services was funded. With such a wider variety of projects and initiatives this is only a brief overview of some of the key projects relevant to this book.

Several projects launched in Phases 1 and 2 are particularly relevant to this book. Projects examining on-demand publishing and electronic reserves were important precursors to the set-up of a national electronic reserve service. Projects such as EDBANK, ERIMS, EUROTEXT, on-Demand Publishing in the Humanities and SCOPE examined on-demand publishing whereas ACORN, ERCOMS, PATRON, QUIPS and ResIDe examined the area of electronic reserves. The issues highlighted by these projects were summarised in an eLib supporting study undertaken in July 1997 to examine the impact of on-demand publishing and electronic reserves (Halliday, 1997). A recurring theme in many of the projects was

the problems associated with traditional short loan collections with '...
ample evidence of unsatisfied demand and indications of hiding, theft,
and vandalism' (Halliday, 1997, p. 125). The advantages of electronic
reserves or on demand publishing were recognised in this report as they
enabled learning resources to be distributed to an increasingly diverse
student population.

Halliday's report recognised that Adobe Acrobat's Portable Document
Format (PDF) was becoming the standard format for delivering
electronic readings. The report concluded by highlighting the challenges
associated with implementing electronic reserves systems and many of
these problems are familiar to librarians involved in such initiatives
today, including:

- obtaining reading lists and in-house produced materials from
  academics;
- a lack of available electronic copies of required texts and the time
  spent scanning;
- running OCR software and proof-reading documents;
- copyright issues.

Copyright was an important issue in each of the projects. Securing
permission to use material for the projects was often relatively
unproblematic; however, publishers were clear that in a real-world
situation charges would be levied. Most publishers based their fees on
usage. The SCOPE Project proposed a fee of 2.5 pence per page, which
was accepted by a large group of publishers, although in general the fees
varied between 2.5 and 5 pence per page. The major problem concerned
the time delay in obtaining permission to use the material. There was
also no clear consensus at the time as to whether copyright charges
should be passed onto students within a digital system. Although some
departments pass on the cost of producing printed study packs to
students, others are fully aware of the hardships students face and
believe core materials should be freely available. A variety of other issues
were also raised by the projects, including whether such systems 'spoon-
feed' students by removing the need to learn how to use library
collections, and the need for lecturer support to make the system viable.
The advantages of online delivery over course packs were examined,
including their importance for distance learning. Issues such as whether
material is designed to be read on screen and the impact this will have
on computing facilities were also considered.

A number of recommendations for the JISC came out of Halliday's report, including recognition of the importance of funding a national electronic reserves service. Consequently, building on the SCOPE and ACORN project, HERON (Higher Education Resources on-demand) was launched in 1998 as part of Phase 3 of the eLib Programme. HERON was jointly funded by JISC and Blackwell's Retail Ltd and built a service for those institutions wishing to progress with on-demand publishing and use electronic text to support learning and teaching in libraries and academic departments. HERON always described itself as a 'project into service' allowing higher education to experiment with both the costs and practicalities of the service in a subsidised environment. HERON offered a copyright clearance and digitisation service and developed a resource bank of digitised materials for use in higher education. It also provided a united voice for higher education in negotiations with publishers and other rights-holders. The start-up service began at the end of May 1999 with initial subscribers offered the options of printed course packs or files for online delivery. JISC continued to fund the service until 2001. The HERON service has very much shaped the nature of electronic reserves services in the UK and is discussed in more detail later in this chapter.

The eLib programme examined many digital library issues and Phase 3 launched in 1998 specifically examined what it termed 'hybrid libraries' as mentioned earlier in this chapter. Five projects were launched within this remit, including BUILDER, AGORA, HyLife, Headline and MALIBU. Rusbridge described the hybrid library as being:

> ... designed to bring a range of technologies from different sources together in the context of a working library, and also to begin to explore integrated systems and services in both the electronic and print environments. The hybrid library should integrate access to all four different kinds of resources identified above, using different technologies from the digital library world, and across different media. (Rusbridge, 1998)

Each project developed a model of the hybrid library using different technical specifications, although often incorporating Z39.50 protocols.[5] The idea was to provide users with 'seamless' access to both electronic and print resources. Access to resources such as electronic journals, library catalogues and networked CD-ROMs was often provided. The BUILDER project was an example of a service that provided access to an electronic short loan collection within the hybrid library environment.[6] Meanwhile the Headline Project had the facility to include course materials, such as lecture notes, alongside library resources.

The hybrid library projects were pioneering and many of the features such as customisation, personalisation and resource sharing are highly relevant to e-learning and are now being incorporated into mainstream library systems and services. All the projects recognised that different groups of users have different needs. Hylife, for example, developed six implementation interfaces for a range of users, including full- and part-time students, researchers, users in distributed environments and various subject groupings.[7] Similarly the Headline Project was very much ahead of its time and enabled users to set up their own Personal Information Environment (PIE) and include a range of different resources within it.[8] This concept is very similar to the 'MyLibrary' approach to customisation that is now offered by library portal software. MALIBU also focused on the needs of users, in particular within the humanities disciplines, and sought to develop 'innovative and cost-effective ways to meet the ever-increasing information requirements of staff and students through co-operative resource-sharing'.[9] The final hybrid library project, AGORA, developed a hybrid library management system (HLMS) to provide integrated access to distributed information services. In parallel with this it also developed library skills materials and experience in the management of hybrid resources. AGORA aimed to increase awareness and understanding of the benefits of a standards-based management framework, and therefore dissemination activities were an important part of the project.

Resource discovery was a major area of research for eLib, and has become extremely important to the success of e-learning, allowing academics and students to identify and access high quality Internet resources. Subject gateways were set up in numerous disciplines, for example OMNI (Online Medical Networked Information) and SOSIG (Social Science Information Gateway) during the early to mid 1990s. These became known as the Resource Discovery Network (RDN) in 1998 and subject gateways were established in many other subject areas so that there are now eight 'hubs'.[10] The RDN is a cooperative network consisting of a central organisation, the Resource Discovery Network Centre (RDNC), and the eight independent service providers. In contrast to search engines, the RDN gathers resources which are carefully selected, indexed and described by specialists in partner institutions. This means that users can be confident that search results and browsing connects them to websites relevant to learning, teaching and research.

The JISC Information Environment (IE)

In 1999 JISC launched the DNER (Distributed National Electronic Resource), which aimed to provide:

> ... a managed environment for accessing quality assured information resources on the Internet which are available from many sources. These resources include scholarly journals, monographs, textbooks, abstracts, manuscripts, maps, music scores, still images, geospatial images and other kinds of vector and numeric data, as well as moving picture and sound collections.[11]

It was envisaged that the DNER would be accessed through a range of different access points, which were termed 'portals'. The DNER interfaces were designed to be distributed, in addition to the distributed nature of the target resources. The main portal types included: the JISC or central portal, subject-oriented portals of the RDN, local portals, media-specific portals, data centre portals, curatorial tradition portals and enriched interface portals. Local portals were hybrid library developments, allowing tailored access to a selection of datasets of importance to an institution, plus integration with other locally licensed datasets and local products. It was argued that systems should be set up to consult local resources first, e.g. the local OPAC or local CD-ROMs, before external or charged services.

The DNER became known as the JISC Information Environment in 2002. JISC were aware that digital library developments may have left users 'bewildered' at the range of resources available and wanted to address this problem. They stated:

> Considerable investment at both the institutional and the national levels has been made to provide high-quality digital information resources for further and higher education. But students, lecturers and researchers are nevertheless currently faced with a vast and sometimes bewildering range of potential sources of electronic information ... little wonder, then, that many users remain unaware of their existence or fail to discover their value for their own learning, teaching or research.[12]

A technical architecture was developed to specify standards and protocols to support the development of integrated resources and allow ease of access for users. Documentation on the JISC IE architecture is available from: *http://www.ukoln.ac.uk/distributed-systems/jisc-ie/arch/*.

These initiatives signified the recognition that the digital library was part of a wider information environment. After 2000, digital library research and development continued to be supported by JISC, although increasingly it examined the role of digital libraries in relation to virtual learning environments. These developments are discussed in Chapter 2.

The digital library today

This section provides an overview of some of the digital library services and systems that are most relevant to this book. Many of the major components of a digital library that can be exploited for e-learning are discussed. These include:

- library portals and digital library management systems;
- electronic reserves;
- digital repositories;
- e-books;
- e-journals;
- reading list management systems;
- e-print repositories.

From OPACS to library portals

Until recently the management of the library collection was primarily undertaken by the library catalogue or library management system (LMS) as they are increasingly known. This is presented to the user as the online public access catalogue (OPAC). OPAC developments have been significant in the last ten years, with most delivered via a web browser and offering users facilities such as inter-library loan, self-service, renewals and, increasingly, integration with the digital library. Many major library management systems have developed modules that, in addition to managing standard library functions such as circulation, serials management, acquisition and ordering, will increasingly manage the digital resources.

In comparing the management of electronic resources to print resources Dempsey (2003) identified some of the problems specifically associated with digital resources, including:

- the variety of formats that makes them less ready to process and present to users than printed materials;
- the different licence conditions that come with digital resources;
- the differing user interfaces associated with them;
- the fact each resource may need individual, customised support.

Moreover, Dempsey argued that the digital environment currently:

> ... lacks consistency; it is as if each book coming into the library was a different shape and had to be read in a different way. The benefits of a more consistent environment are clear: library time and resource should be freed to think about selection and use of the collection, not consumed by the messy mechanics of acquisition and processing; and the user experience should be shaped by learning and research needs not by the arbitrary constraints of interface and format. (Dempsey, 2003, p. 5)

Library portals are one response to these problems and provide intermediate layers between users and resources in an attempt to manage and provide access to the diverse wealth of electronic resources available. The portal aims to overcome the fragmentation of digital resources, presenting the user with a unified interface rather than the individual characteristics of different services or systems. Nevertheless, Dempsey (2003) also stated that the word portal is one of the least helpful terms coined in recent years. He presented two definitions of the term, the first as an information hub or entry point to electronic resources. In the second he suggested that a portal is the way in which a library mediates the engagement of users and resources in a networked environment. Portals are not exclusive to the library community and JISC have been developing different types of portals for different purposes. They define a portal as:

> ... a network service that brings together content from diverse distributed resources using technologies such as cross searching, harvesting, and alerting, and collate this into an amalgamated form for presentation to the user.[13]

Currently research is being undertaken at Loughborough University to investigate library portals. The LibPortal Project argues that:

> The adoption of locally developed and commercial library portals in academic institutions is having a profound impact on the use of

quality information sources, as well as on internal library workflows and efficiency. Library portals will be crucial to interoperation with national services and institutional portal and VLE [virtual learning environment] developments.[14]

The development of electronic reserves

A growing number of academic libraries provide electronic access to core readings, and in the US in particular, electronic reserves services, as they are known, have been running for a number of years. In the UK, the services are generally known as electronic short loan, electronic course packs or electronic off-print services. However, the principle is the same: core readings are copyright cleared (where necessary), scanned and made available to users via a network. For the purposes of this book the term electronic reserves is used to include all the above services. Nevertheless, this is an area where very little research has been undertaken and most of the literature is based on anecdotal evidence. The Association of Research Libraries (ARL) have run a mailing list on the topic since 1994 and this list has seen a steady number of postings. In addition, the *Journal of InterLibrary Loan and Document Delivery* includes electronic reserves within its remit and has published a number of special editions dedicated to the topic. However, in the UK, the expansion of such services has been slow because of the need to obtain copyright clearance for all materials. Developments have been largely led by JISC initiatives and in particular the launch of a national service, HERON, now run by Ingenta UK.

Universities adopt a variety of approaches towards providing access to core readings in electronic format, and the marked differences between the US, UK and Australia are largely shaped by copyright law in the respective countries, which is discussed in more detail in Chapter 4. Some universities have developed their own in-house electronic reserve· system. In-house systems have the obvious advantage that they can be tailored to meet the needs of individual organisations and can be as sophisticated or as simple as the budget allows. Electronic reserves can also be developed using features within library management systems, e.g. the 'reserves' module within the Voyager library management system. Software developers have also realised the growth in interest in this area and a number of ready-made electronic reserves systems are also available, such as ERes. A seemingly unlimited combination of these approaches is also possible, such as linking ERes to WebCT, or the Voyager reserve module to Blackboard. Of the software that is available, Docutek Information Systems' ERes package (which recently launched version 4) is the most popular in the US. It is designed to allow academic libraries to establish Electronic Reserves and to manage copyright-protected documents online.[15] Together with other modules in the DocuLib suite, libraries can compile and manage collections of Internet resources, post time-sensitive information, and create and administer surveys online. DocuLib and ERes can also be used to create course websites, course-specific discussion boards and live Internet chat rooms.

US electronic reserves

Electronic reserves systems were established in many US academic libraries in the 1990s, e.g. in North Western University Library, Illinois.[16] The Library has integrated its short loan collection, known as 'reserved readings', into their library catalogue, which uses the Voyager Library System. A combination of lecture notes, articles and readings for courses are also included on the system. Access is limited to members of the university using an authentication system to prevent external users from gaining access to copyright controlled material in the collection. Similarly, San Diego State University operates an electronic course reserves (ECR) system using the ERes software, which provides a ready-made electronic reserve delivery system.[17] As well as the electronic reserves system, ERes contains lists of useful websites and chat areas for staff and students. Lecturers are able to add material by e-mailing the ECR coordinator. Care is taken to operate within the copyright legislation and the system is only available to members of the University. Within these systems, files are usually stored in Portable Document Format (PDF) and accessed using browser software such as Netscape with Adobe Acrobat Reader. An example of this approach is Duke University, where the Electronic Reserves system provides access to supplementary course reading materials required in support of the curriculum.[18] To obtain a copy of scanned documents, printing must be undertaken using a system supporting PDF. Copyright law in the US is such that many librarians allow material to be placed on electronic reserve for one year without requiring copyright permission. This is undertaken through the Fair Use clause (see Chapter 4, pp. 82–3 for more detail).

Australia

In Australia, the development of electronic reserves was problematic until 2001 when the copyright law was changed to allow core readings to be scanned for educational use. This was to be undertaken under licence from the Copyright Agency Limited (CAL), Australia's reprographic rights organisation, which operates in a similar manner to the UK's Copyright Licensing Agency (CLA) and offers licences that allow authorised copying at different types of establishment. The Electronic Reproduction and Communication Licence covers reproduction in an electronic form (e.g. digital to digital) and communication of copies in electronic form (e.g. posting copies on an intranet). Following this change in the law, electronic reserve systems were established in many academic libraries. An example is the University of South Australia which set up a Digital Resource Management Centre to provide central record keeping of all print materials that are digitised to support the University's teaching and learning programmes.[19] Similarly, Adelaide University established the Digital Resources Management Centre as part of an initiative by the University Library, the Division of the University Secretary and the Learning and Teaching Development Unit. It was set up to monitor the production of copyright material in digital format and to ensure compliance with copyright legislation.

Electronic reserves in the UK

The development of electronic reserves projects in UK academic libraries has been shaped by the eLib programme which, through projects such as ACORN and SCOPE, discussed earlier in this chapter, demonstrated the need for such services and the technical capabilities to provide it. The launch of the HERON (Higher Education Resources on-demand) Project, which subsequently became first a JISC-funded then a commercial service, has allowed many universities to outsource the associated copyright clearance and digitisation work. However, despite many local and national initiatives since the early 1990s, the restrictive nature of UK copyright law and the inadequate provision of a scalable licensing model for digital texts have meant that electronic reserves have generally remained small scale and been based on pilot projects.

Electronic reserves are discussed in more detail in Chapter 6, which includes a case study from a UK university which has managed to introduce significant electronic reserve services. There is a considerable body of experience in the UK community; however, this currently lies almost exclusively within the HERON User Group and on the private mailing list for HERON members.

E-books

The term e-book has a variety of meanings, but generally it applies to published materials, such as reference books or monographs, that have been converted into digital format for electronic distribution. E-books offer significant advantages to the learner with improved access to reading material, 24 hours a day, from any location. It is possible to download many e-books to personal digital assistants (PDAs) or other handheld devices making them truly portable. From the perspective of libraries, e-books do not require shelf space in the library and cannot be damaged or removed from the collection like a physical book. Some of the first e-books were launched by start-up companies who struck deals with academic and commercial publishers to make their reading material available. There are now significant numbers of traditional publishers offering e-book services to libraries or directly to the public. In addition to this there has been significant investment of public and private money into digitising out-of-copyright works, including many classic texts and making them freely available on the Internet.

Project Gutenberg maintains that it is the Internet's oldest producer of free e-books, being started in 1971 by Michael Hart at the University of Illinois who first typed in the American Declaration of Independence.[20] Starting in 1991, Project Gutenberg began to take its current form, with many different texts being added and targets defined. The target for 1991 was one book a month. 1992's target was two books a month. This target doubled every year through 1996, when it hit 32 books a month. Currently the Project has a target of 400 books a month. The present collection of more than 10,000 e-books was produced by hundreds of volunteers. Most of the Project Gutenberg 'eBooks' are older literary works that are in the public domain in the United States. All may be freely downloaded and read, and redistributed for non-commercial use.

Free e-books are also available from numerous other sources and the Internet Public Library maintains a list of online texts.[21] The Electronic Text Center at the University of Virginia was established in 1992 and currently includes approximately 70,000 on- and off-line humanities texts in 13 languages, with more than 350,000 related images (book illustrations, covers, manuscripts, newspaper pages, page images of

Special Collections books, museum objects, etc.). They currently provide access to over 1,800 e-books in Microsoft Reader format.

In the UK, e-books were part of a major study funded by JISC, EBONI (Electronic Books on-screen Interface) which ran for 20 months from August 2000.[22] JISC subsequently set up an e-books Working Group, which published a paper in 2001 examining the associated issues (Woodward and Edwards, 2001). The paper provides a useful overview of the major issues.

Commerical e-book services

NetLibrary was one of the first e-book services, launched in 1998 as a division of OCLC.[23] It offers services to academic, public, special and corporate libraries, aiming in many ways to mimic a traditional library service. Subscribing institutions purchase a collection of titles in a similar way to printed titles; however, the electronic collection is hosted with netLibrary on their servers. Library users can then find e-books through MARC records in the library catalogue. As with printed books, only one user at a time may access each copy of an e-book and the library determines the loan period. At the time of writing, over 40,000 e-books were available through netLibrary from publishers such as McGraw-Hill, MIT Press and Oxford University Press. The significant drawback to netLibrary is their model, which allows only one user to access a book at any one time. However, netLibrary is currently reviewing different access models that meet both library demands and publisher needs.

Questia was another of the early e-book companies launched in 1999; however, it is marketed at students, with librarians employed on collection-building.[24] The Questia service went live in early 2001 and claimed to hold at least 50,000 of the most valued volumes in the liberal arts from the twentieth and twenty-first centuries (not including textbooks). Questia has been called 'the world's largest online library of books' and in 2003 the company had over 400,000 titles available from over 200 publishers, including Pearson and several university presses. Anyone can search Questia at no cost to locate books and journals, but to view full text online and access the research tools of the Questia service users must subscribe. Questia offers students search facilities and also tools to make notes in books they own, create personal bookshelves and create formatted footnotes and bibliographies using a variety of citation styles.

Many UK publishers, such as Oxford University Press and Taylor & Francis, have launched e-book deals available through the Combined Higher Education Software Team (CHEST). Universities have recently signed up to commercial e-book suppliers and study reading lists to see how many core textbooks would be available. Currently, many companies are still geared towards the US market but e-books should be considered when planning any new electronic service.

Electronic journals

No discussion of the digital library would be complete without considering the enormous changes that the journal publishing industry has undergone in the last ten years and the impact this has had on serials management in libraries. Electronic journals in all subjects are now widely available and the pricing and licensing models are now becoming established. Many publications are available examining this subject in far greater detail, e.g. Fowler (2004) and Kidd and Rees-Jones (2000). Electronic journals can take the form of electronic versions of printed journals, usually available in conjunction with a subscription to a printed title, or electronic only publications. Some are freely available, but often titles require subscription. Titles can also be bought directly from publishers, or via an aggregator, such as Swetswise or Ingenta. These variations in purchasing arrangements and publishing models can all make serials management increasingly complex, and ensuring library users have access to the full range of electronic journal titles can be challenging. Traditionally, libraries have managed access to journals from title links in the OPAC or by setting up electronic journals access pages. Increasingly, larger academic libraries are moving towards using serials management systems, of which there are a number of commercial products available. However, in this area in particular, building links between e-learning systems and library resources is crucial.

Recent research has suggested that academic staff and students are becoming increasingly comfortable with the use of electronic journals for teaching and research because of the obvious advantages of access. Bonthron et al. (2003), in a recent study of trends in the use of electronic journals in higher education, noted differences between the subject disciplines, but found that that generally academic staff were not using library electronic journal pages, and were inclined to bookmark their favourite e-journal sites. Drawing on findings from the JISC Usage Surveys: Trends in Electronic Information Services (JUSTEIS) Project,[25]

Bonthron reported similar findings for e-journal usage of undergraduate students. Their usage is primarily directed by their lecturer and undergraduates use links from their course website or the VLE, but are also less likely to use library electronic journals pages. The paper reports:

> The library manager may have to decide where to allocate effort – into library web pages which may be used intermittently if at all, or into support of academic staff and learning support staff in development of VLEs. (Bonthron, 2003)

The use and value of electronic journals to research and teaching is undoubted, but this is an area that highlights the need for integration, not just between systems, but also between communities of practitioners. Librarians increasingly need to be part of a wider group of learning support staff and this issue is examined in more detail in Chapter 3.

E-print services

What are they?

A study by Halliday and Oppenheim (2001) examined the development of electronic journals, reviewing cost and pricing developments and concluded that there appears to be no relationship between production costs and the subscription prices of scholarly journals. They argue that journals are priced according to what the market will bear, but, at the same time, the market is inelastic. As a result, prices have consistently increased annually at a rate well above the general inflation rate for the last two decades. These changes have been referred to as a 'serials crisis' or crisis in scholarly communication and it has been the impetus for a number of developments that aim to use digital technology to reduce costs for the higher education sector. Developments include alternative models of journal production, such as the setting up of institutional repositories, and initiatives that aim to influence the structure of the market for scholarly journals with a view to driving prices down such as the Scholarly Publishing and Academic Resources Coalition (SPARC).

SPARC was formed in the United States in 1998 by the Association of Research Libraries (ARL) as a movement to counteract this commercialisation and stranglehold that publishers have on scholarly publishing. The movement is an alliance of universities, research libraries and organisations. SPARC argues that market dysfunctions in the scholarly communication system have reduced the dissemination of scholarship and crippled libraries. However, some commentators like Professor Stevan Harnad[26] believe that, rather than a frontal attack on commercial publishers, open archives should be established. Authors should deposit their research output in e-print repositories at their own institutions and data from these repositories can be harvested globally.

Why are they valuable?

JISC recognised that there are numerous internal and external advantages of e-print repositories to institutions, including benefits:

- to researchers through wider and more rapid dissemination of their work, resulting in more 'research impact';
- to students, as university publications are readily accessible via the institution's virtual learning environment, library system and institutional portal;
- to the university from a higher profile by making all output publicly (and freely) available. Additionally, the university benefits by having a comprehensive, managed and preserved record of its research output, instantly available for research assessment or related exercises;
- e-print repositories offer clear advantages to e-learning, as they allow valuable institutional resources to be made available without licensing or copyright issues. They are also significant as these initiatives are usually led by librarians. This gives the profession an important role in communicating the benefits to the academic community.

E-prints in the US, UK and Australia

These developments have led to a growing interest in the US, UK and Australia in the set-up of institutional e-print repositories. One of the world's leading open-source initiatives is at the Massachusetts Institute of Technology (MIT) with its DSpace Project,[27] a digital repository to capture, distribute and preserve MIT's intellectual output. MIT stated that these archives may provide more efficient open access to research than the commercial journals.

In the UK, numerous projects, again funded largely by JISC, have been established to explore the technical aspects of setting up e-print archives and the wider implications for higher education. Several of these projects

have been funded under the Focus on Access to Institutional Resources (FAIR) Programme[28] and ePrints UK[29] is one such project funded for two years and due for completion in July 2004. The project is developing a series of national, discipline-focused services through which the higher and further education community can access the collective output of e-print papers. These will be available from compliant open archive repositories, particularly those provided by UK universities and colleges. JISC also funded the SHERPA (Securing a Hybrid Environment for Research Preservation and Access) Initiative[30] under the FAIR Programme, which is investigating issues regarding the development of openly accessible institutional digital repositories in universities. The University of Southampton has been leading much of the developments with the Open Citation Project.

Developments in Australia were led by the Australian National University (ANU), following an initiative by the university librarian, Colin Steele. Steele published an account of developments to date (Steele, 2002) and described how the first e-print repository was established at ANU on 1 September 2001. By August 2002 the repository held 317 'documents' covering material from pre-prints to refereed articles and from conference papers to books. In 2002, a 'roadshow' was funded and led by key staff at ANU to explain, facilitate and promote the concept of e-print repositories. Following this, initiatives were established at the University of Queensland, Sydney and others.

Open Archives Initiative (OAI)

An important development that has its roots in the development of e-print archives is the Open Archives Initiative (OAI).[31] The OAI develops and promotes interoperability standards that aim to facilitate the efficient dissemination of content. This is discussed in more detail in Chapter 5.

Reading list management systems

Reading list management has been a problem for academic libraries for many years, both in ensuring that up-to-date lists of resources are received by the library for acquisition purposes, and that students obtain access to these resources. Currently, this seems to be a key area where the synergies between digital libraries and e-learning systems are most apparent. Several major library management system vendors have developed reading list modules to help solve this problem. In addition, a number of new companies have established reading list management systems which integrate with both library management systems and e-learning software.

Reading lists are also increasingly being seen not simply as lists of books in the library, but as resource lists, which point to resources in no matter what format. So a resource list can include books and journals held in printed format that need to be consulted in the library, but also electronic journals which can be accessed through an institutional subscription, or a web page available for students to download. Reading lists featured in several of the Digital Library and Virtual Learning Environments (DiVLE) projects and were the primary focus of the DELIVER (Digital Electronic Library Integrating Virtual EnviRonments) Project. This is discussed in more detail in Chapter 2.

Sheffield University Library has reading lists for certain departments mounted on the library website. These are then linked to the university catalogue, which uses Talis software. More information is provided in Chapter 6 about this example. John Rylands University Library of Manchester also has reading lists linked to their library catalogue, again using the Talis software. At John Rylands a wide range of departments have provided reading lists for many different courses. Course material is also available, such as essay questions, although this varies depending on individual lecturers. Where material is available as a website this is linked directly from the reading list. Electronic journals are also linked from the OPAC, so users can access some course material directly. A different approach is taken at Aberdeen University which has what is known as a 'course handbook library'. This is an electronic library of student handbooks and other course material provided by teaching departments. It is intended to be used for backup and reference purposes, as most of the documents included in the library are handed out or offered for sale within the relevant courses. Some of the material in this database is only open to members of Aberdeen University and access is controlled by password. Not all course material is available via the library and it is the responsibility of individual lecturers to tell students when material is held on the departmental website.

Conclusion

This chapter has provided an overview of the development of digital libraries from the early 1990s. The chapter first examined key research and development in the area, including the work of the JISC in the UK and the NSF in the US. The second part of the chapter provided an overview of some key digital library services and systems, such as electronic journals, e-books, electronic reserves and library portals. The chapter includes many developments, which may be familiar to librarians, but sets the scene for the remainder of the book. Chapter 2 considers e-learning and how this has developed in parallel with the digital library. An important aspect of Chapter 2 is concerned with how, since 2000, e-learning and digital libraries have become increasingly interlinked, and how in the future the importance of integration between both systems and the communities of support staff will become essential.

Notes

1. Cornell Institute for Digital Collections. Hp. Cornell University. Available from: *http://cidc.library.cornell.edu/*.

2. Paul Conway. *Project Open Book*. Hp. Yale University. Available from: *http://www.library.yale.edu/preservation/pobweb.htm*.

3. *Digital Libraries Inititative*. Hp. 25 June 1999 [last update]. Online. National Science Foundation. Available from: *http://www.dli2.nsf.gov/*.

4. International Digital Libraries Programme website. Available from: *http://www.jisc.ac.uk/index.cfm?name=programme_nsf*

5. Z39.50 refers to the International Standard, ISO 23950: 'Information Retrieval (Z39.50): Application Service Definition and Protocol Specification', and to ANSI/NISO Z39.50. It specifies a client–server-based protocol for searching and retrieving information from remote databases. This is discussed in more detail in Chapter 5.

6. The BUILDER Project (Birmingham University Integrated Library Development and Electronic Resource). See: *http://builder.bham.ac.uk/main.asp*.

7. More details available from: *http://hylife.unn.ac.uk/*

8. More details available from: *http://www.headline.ac.uk/*

9. Taken from Project Malibu home page: *http://www.kcl.ac.uk/humanities/cch/malibu/background/intro.htm* (November 2000).

10. RDN website: *http://www.rdn.ac.uk/*

11. JISC website: *http://www.jisc.ac.uk/dner/* October 2000.

12. *Investing in the Future: Developing an Online Information Environment*. Available from: *http://www.jisc.ac.uk/index.cfm?name=ie_home*

13. Portals: Frequently Asked Questions. Available from: *http://www.jisc.ac.uk/ index.cfm?name=ie_portalsfaq*

14. See: *http://www.lboro.ac.uk/departments/dils/lisu/portals.html*

15. See: *http://www.docutek.com/*

16. See: *http://www.library.nwu.edu/ERS/*

17. See: *http://ecr.sdsu.edu/*

18. See: *http://www.lib.duke.edu/access/reserves/*

19. See: *http://www.library.unisa.edu.au/drmc/default.asp*

20. See: *http://gutenberg.net/*

21. See: *http://www.ipl.org/div/subject/browse/hum60.60.00/*

22. See: *http://ebooks.cis.strath.ac.uk/eboni/overview.html*

23. See: *http://www.netlibrary.com/*

24. See: *http://www.questia.com/*

25. See: *http://www.dil.aber.ac.uk/dils/research/justeis/jisctop.htm*

26. See, for example: *http://www.nature.com/nature/debates/e-access/Articles/ harnad.html*

27. See: *http://www.dspace.org/live/home.html*

28. See: *http://www.jisc.ac.uk/index.cfm?name=programme_fair*

29. See: *http://www.rdn.ac.uk/projects/eprints-uk/*

30. See: *http://www.sherpa.ac.uk*

31. See: *http://www.openarchives.org/*

References

Bonthron, Karen et al. (2003) 'Trends in use of electronic journals in higher education in the UK – views of academic staff and students', *D-Lib Magazine*, 9(6).

Borgman, C. (2003) *From Gutenberg to the Global Information Infrastructure: Access to Information in the Networked World.* Cambridge, MA: MIT Press.

Carpenter, Leona, Shaw, Simon and Prescott, Andrew (eds) (1998) *Towards the Digital Library: The British Library's 'Initiatives for Access' Programme.* London: British Library.

Castells, Manuel (1996) *The Rise of the Network Society.* London: Blackwells.

Crawford, Walt and Gorman, Michael (1995) *Future Libraries: Dreams, Madness and Reality.* Chicago: ALA.

DELOS (2001) *Digital libraries: future directions for a European research programme.* Available from: *http://www.dli2.nsf .gov/internationalprojects/eu_future.html.*

Dempsey, Lorcan (2003) *The recombinant library: portals and people.* Available from: *http://www.oclc.org/research/staff/dempsey/dempsey_ recombinant_library.pdf.*

Fowler, David (2004) *E-Serials Collection Management: Transitions, Trends and Technicalities.* Haworth Press.

Halliday, L. and Oppenheim, C. (2001) 'Developments in digital journals', *Journal of Documentation,* 57(2), 260–83.

Halliday, Leah (ed.) (1997) *The Impact of on-Demand Publishing and Electronic Reserve on Student Teaching and Libraries in the UK: A Supporting Study in the JISC Electronic Libraries (eLib) Programme.* London: LITC South Bank University.

HEFCE (1993) *Joint funding Council's libraries review group: Report* (The Follett Report). December 1993. Available from: *http://www .ukoln.ac.uk/services/papers/follett/report/.*

Kidd, Tony and Rees-Jones, Lyndsay (eds) (2000) *The Serials Management Handbook: A Practical Guide to Print and Electronic Serials Management.* London: Library Association Publishing.

Lang, Brian (1998) 'Developing the digital library', in Leona Carpenter, Simon Shaw and Andrew Prescott (eds), *Towards the Digital Library: The British Library's 'Initiatives for Access' Programme.* London: British Library.

Lesk, Michael (1997) *Practical Digital Libraries: Books, Bytes and Bucks,* Morgan Kaufmann Series in Multimedia Information & Systems. San Francisco: Morgan Kaufmann.

LIC (1997) *New Library: The People's Network.* London: Library and Information Commission. Chairman: Matthew Evans. Available from: *http://www.ukoln.ac.uk/services/lic/newlibrary/.*

Martin, William J. (1995) *The Global Information Society,* 1st edn. Aldershot: Gower. Quoted in: Martin, William J. (1998) *The Global Information Society,* 2nd edn. Aldershot: Gower.

Ogg, Harold C. and Ogg, Marlene H. (1992) *Optical Character Recognition: A Librarian's Guide.* Westport, CT: Meckler.

Rusbridge, Chris (1998) 'Towards the hybrid library', *D-lib magazine,* July/August. Available from: *http://mirrored.ukoln.ac.uk/lis-journals/ dlib/dlib/dlib/july98/rusbridge/07rusbridge.html.*

Secker, Jane (2001) *Access to core course materials project: Final Report.* Available from: *http://www.ucl.ac.uk/epd/tqef/core/final.pdf.*

E-learning and the digital library

Introduction

This chapter first examines the development of e-learning and specifically virtual learning environments (VLEs). In the US, as previously noted, these systems are often referred to as learning management systems (LMS). It discusses developments from the early 1990s through to July 2003, when the UK's Department for Education and Skills published its consultation document that aimed to establish an e-learning strategy for the whole education sector. The chapter shows how e-learning developments initially took place in parallel to the digital library initiatives outlined in Chapter 1. It goes on to describe how the work of the e-learning community and the library community first became aligned, and then integrally linked. Arguably, integration between these two types of systems is now paramount to the success of future developments. Much has been written about e-learning and this chapter can only hope to be a broad summary. However, further reading is suggested throughout and references are available at the end of the chapter. The chapter focuses specifically on developments in UK higher education because a significant body of research on VLE and library integration has been undertaken.

E-learning has become a familiar term, but if asked to define exactly what it means many librarians may struggle. Computers have been used in education since the personal computer was invented. However, for many years computers were used as a tool to aid learning in an uncoordinated and unmanaged way, or students were simply taught to use computers for practical reasons: to learn how to use word processors or develop databases or spreadsheets. Most students will have been educated through conventional, face-to-face teaching and while they may have learnt to use numerous computer packages, much of their education will have been classroom based and of the 'chalk and talk' nature. In contrast, children today are exposed to computers for education purposes from their first entry into education. In further and higher education the use of learning management software is commonplace, but children as young as six or seven are also familiar with using computers in the classroom, accessing the Internet, visiting virtual chat rooms and using messenger software to communicate with their friends.

As with developments in the digital library field, UK Higher Education Funding Councils and the Joint Information Systems Committee (JISC), have been instrumental in bringing about change in this area, with programmes designed to support and encourage change, such as the Teaching and Learning Technologies Programme (TLTP) and the Fund for the Development of Teaching and Learning (FDTL). With a view to the focus of this book and its target audience, this chapter moves on to consider e-learning and libraries. A detailed overview of the JISC Digital Libraries and Virtual Learning Environments (DiVLE) Programme is provided. The chapter also demonstrates that libraries are more widely recognised as playing an important role in e-learning, as evidenced by the establishment of the OCLC e-Learning Task Force and their recent White Paper examining *Libraries and the enhancement of e-learning.*

The concept of e-learning and learning technologies

E-learning is a term with a variety of meanings. To add to the confusion, terms such as 'learning technology' and 'educational technology' also exist, with differing meanings. The UK's Department for Education and Skills (DfES) defines e-learning in very broad terms, and its definition issued in 2003 stated:

> If someone is learning in a way that uses information and communication technologies (ICTs), they are using e-learning. (DfES, 2003, p.4)

The DfES argues:

> E-learning has the power to transform the way we learn, and to bring high quality, accessible learning to everyone – so that every learner can achieve his or her full potential. (DfES, 2003, p. 1)

The UK government's e-learning Strategy Unit is headed by one of the key researcher's in the field Diana Laurillard. Laurillard, the former Professor of Educational Technology at the Open University, has written widely on the subject of technology and student learning since the late 1970s – see, for example, Laurillard (1979) and Laurillard (1991). More recently, her book *Rethinking University Teaching* (Laurillard, 1993) has received widespread recognition with the second edition being published in 2002. She elaborates what is known as 'Conversational Theory' first developed by Gordon Pask, the cybernetician, in the 1970s. Conversational Theory regards teaching and learning as an iterative process and Laurillard also drew on learning theories developed by Vygotsky to develop her 'Conversational Framework'. This framework is based on a dialogue between the teacher and student, although this need not be direct face-to-face discussion. Before considering technology, Laurillard presents a notion of learning and teaching as a dialogue, where one-to-one tutorials are the ideal teaching situation. She then goes on to examine ways in which learning technologies can support aspects of this conversational framework.

Other key authors on UK learning technology include Gilly Salmon, who has written more specifically on using computer-mediated communication for teaching and learning (Salmon, 2002). It is significant that in the UK these two researchers originate from the Open University, which, as the UK's leading distance education institution, has been instrumental in using technology for educational purposes.

In the US the term 'educational technology' is used more widely and although education is generally provided at a state level, the US Department of Education set up the Office of Educational Technology in the late 1990s. The Office develops US educational technology policy and implements this policy through educational technology programmes. More specifically it aims to:

> Provide leadership to the nation in using technology to promote achievement of the National Education Goals and to increase opportunities for all students.[1]

In March 2004 Susan Patrick was appointed director of the Office of Educational Technology. She is responsible for coordinating programmes and policies on virtual education and e-learning. Her office defines educational technology as:

> A variety of electronic tools, media, and environments that can be used to enhance learning, foster creativity, stimulate communication, encourage collaboration, and engage in the continuous development and application of knowledge and skills.[2]

An important global organisation is EDUCAUSE, which is a not-for-profit association aiming to advance higher education by promoting the intelligent use of information technology. Membership is open to institutions of higher education, corporations serving the higher education information technology market, and other related associations and organisations. It has a global membership in over 30 countries, although the vast majority of its members are from the United States. While this organisation is not specifically focused on e-learning, it hosts an annual conference which provides an important global forum for the exchange of ideas and e-learning and is very much at the forefront of these ideas. Their definition is as follows:

> Electronic learning denotes learning environments consisting of hardware, software and personnel; a multi-faceted learning program that utilises distance learning, interactive cable TV, and the Internet to connect learning environments to homes, places of work, and the community at large.[3]

E-learning – where did it come from?

This section traces the development of e-learning since the 1980s. In his paper on e-learning, Appelmans (2002) characterised the development of e-learning in four phases, including:

- Instructor-led Training Era (pre-1983)
- Multimedia Era (1984–93)
- First Wave e-Learning (1994–99)
- Second Wave e-Learning (2000–beyond).

Many of the developments were shaped by advances in technology, and in particular by the development of the Internet. During what Appelmans calls the Instructor-Led Training Era, computers were not widely available in offices, homes or educational institutions and so much computer-based learning was instructor led in a specific room.

From my own experiences I think back to a computer literacy course that was taught on BBC microcomputers in a specially installed suite in the college. Activities were based solely in the classroom and there was no opportunity to practise the skills we learnt outside of the classroom.

During the mid-1980s to the mid-1990s there were a number of technological advances, including the development of the Windows operating system, CD-ROMs and desktop software such as PowerPoint. CD-ROMs meant that computer-based training could be delivered remotely and there were attempts to make the materials more visually engaging. In the UK during this period, the higher education funding bodies launched a number of funding programmes such as the Teaching and Learning Technologies Programme (TLTP). These are discussed in more detail later in the chapter.

From the mid to late 1990s e-learning began to take off as the Web evolved. Other significant developments included the widespread use of e-mail, web browsers and media players. The use of computer conferencing first became significant during this period; for example, the Open University adopted the FirstClass Conferencing System. However, without sufficient network capabilities, much of these developments were limited and the potential for e-learning was not fully achieved. Applemans regards the period from 2000 onwards as being the second wave of e-learning with significant technological advances, in particular high bandwidth capabilities. Streaming media and advanced website design has revolutionised the education sector. Most significantly during this period is the widespread adoption in further and higher education of virtual learning environment software, which is discussed below.

The importance of communication to the learning process has been recognised for many years and during the late 1980s and early 1990s computer conferencing initiatives began to be set up. The FirstClass conferencing system has been used at the Open University since the early 1990s to support distance-learning students. In 1996 it was also adopted by the University of Wales, Aberystwyth, to support its distance-learning programmes in librarianship and information studies.

I was involved in an early use of bulletin board technology in 1990, when several schools in Hertfordshire (UK) were set up to encourage A-level students to discuss problems and issues and to assist their studies.

E-learning or learning technology has also developed as an academic discipline and is grounded in and draws upon several fields of research. This is not discussed in this book in any great detail; however, librarians and information professionals should be aware that while many of those involved in e-learning are practitioners, a body of researchers exist in the field. Their work often draws on research from psychology and from educational theorists such as Pask, Vygotsky and Kolb. Various theories of learning have also shaped the development of e-learning, which include behaviourism, cognitivism and constructivism. The Association for Learning Technology (ALT) has a learning technology theory special interest group[4] and the ALT journal, *ALT-J*, argues strongly for research in the field to be supported by theory. Writers such as Oliver (2000) and Conole and Oliver (2002) have advocated that practitioners need to develop a greater understanding of such theories.

E-learning, distance education and blended learning

E-learning also has close associations with the development of distance learning and its potential to reach learners any time, any place is one of its key attractions. The development of the Internet and associated communication technologies has led many universities to start offering distance-learning programmes, particularly at postgraduate level. Computer-mediated communication (CMC) was one of the first technologies used to replicate the social interaction of the classroom, missing from many distance programmes. However, increasingly the term e-learning is seen as an integral part of the support offered to campus-based students. The use of both traditional and technology-supported learning is referred to by some as 'blended learning'. It is important to remember that e-learning facilitates distance learning, but is not always something delivered to those at a distance.

UK developments in learning technology

The UK higher education funding bodies have been instrumental in supporting developments in teaching and learning technologies. Starting in the early 1990s, programmes such as TLTP and the Fund for the Development of Teaching and Learning (FDTL) have been launched to kick-start developments in this area.

The Teaching and Learning Technologies Programme and the Fund for the Development of Teaching and Learning

TLTP began in 1992, supported by the four funding bodies. Seventy-six projects were funded under the first two phases, which aimed to introduce, support and develop new technology-based teaching and learning materials. In 1996, the funding bodies commissioned a consortium led by Coopers & Lybrand to evaluate the programme. The findings indicated the need to concentrate more on implementation and embedding of materials within institutions. The higher education funding councils therefore initiated Phase 3 of TLTP, with funding of £3.5 million a year for three years. Most projects were for implementation, to increase the use of technology-based materials in teaching and learning. Four projects are to develop new materials.

In 1999, following the success of the first and second phases of the Teaching and Learning Technology Programme (TLTP), the Higher Education Funding Council for England (HEFCE) commissioned a study to examine the use of TLTP materials in higher education in the UK.[5] The study demonstrated that TLTP materials have been adopted throughout UK higher education. They were embedded in conventional courses, alongside a very substantial use of other types of communication and information technologies.

Meanwhile the Fund for the Development of Teaching and Learning (FDTL) was launched by the HEFCE and the Department of Education, Northern Ireland (DENI) in December 1995. The aims of the FDTL were to:

- stimulate developments in learning and teaching;
- secure the widest possible involvement of institutions in the take-up and implementation of good practice.

While this funding strand was not associated specifically with technology, arguably it was another important mechanism for initiating change. Funds were awarded to projects that showed the potential to make a contribution to the development and improvement of learning and teaching through the transfer of information and ideas. This was the first time the results of the quality assessment process were linked to the allocation of funds to the higher education sector. Phase 1 covered the 15 subjects assessed under the quality assessment method used between February 1993 and June 1995. Forty-four projects were funded at a cost of £8.5 million. In December 1996 bids under Phase 2 were invited. This phase covered eight subjects including: chemical engineering, sociology, linguistics, French, German and related languages, Italian, Iberian languages and studies, and Russian and Eastern European languages and studies. Nineteen projects were funded at a cost of £4 million. The majority of these projects started in October 1997 and ran for three years.

Phase 3 of this programme was launched in 1999 and a total of 33 projects were funded, at a total cost of £6.8 million over three years. Phase 4 of the FDTL covered the 13 subject areas assessed by the Quality Assurance Agency for Higher Education in the period October 1998 to September 2000. The aims of Phase 4 of the FDTL are to stimulate developments in learning and teaching and to secure the widest possible involvement of institutions in the take-up and implementation of good practice.

The Dearing Report

However, the real impetus for change arguably came in July 1997 when the National Committee of Inquiry into Higher Education (NCIHE, 1997) produced what is commonly known as the Dearing Report. The report made recommendations for the development of higher education over the next 20 years and recognised that communication and information technology was central to the progression of the national education system. Dearing maintained that:

> Communication and information technology holds out much promise for improving the quality, flexibility and effectiveness of higher education. (NCIHE, 1997)

In particular, innovative application of technology was highlighted and it claimed that the potential benefits would 'extend to, and affect the practice of, learning and teaching research'. In many ways this report was the catalyst for ongoing efforts to embed learning technologies in education in the UK.

Teaching Quality Enhancement Fund

As part of the HEFCE strategy, all higher education institutions are encouraged to strive towards excellence, not just in research, but in teaching and learning. Building on the work of the FDTL to further the development of high-quality teaching, institutions were encouraged by central government to develop strategy documents in this area. The Teaching Quality Enhancement Fund (TQEF), launched in 1999, was specifically designed to support institutions in the implementation of their Teaching and Learning Strategy. Following a consultation across higher education, 'many argued that an institution-wide approach, underpinned by a clear strategy [was] central to developing teaching excellence' (HEFCE, 1999). TQEF funds were put to a variety of uses in different institutions, with some universities choosing to fund specialist projects and others putting the money towards wider initiatives.

In 2001 the HEFCE undertook a detailed analysis of institutional teaching and learning strategies (Gibbs, 2001). Gibbs examined how teaching and learning strategies had developed in the period from 1998 to 2001. In particular, Gibbs recognised that teaching and learning strategies had improved significantly during this period and contained more of the components expected in a strategy document. Some important components are identified as operational plans, change mechanisms and means of monitoring. Specific targets that specify outputs and particularly outcomes for students are also recognised as being important components in a strategy. Gibbs recognised that plans for evaluation are frequently absent from Teaching and Learning Strategies and few pay attention to changing the 'teaching culture' or 'addressing institutional blocks'. Gibbs was also concerned that while innovations were being encouraged at almost all institutions, these were not being embedded into the organisation.

The development of virtual learning environments

The term 'virtual learning environment' was first coined in the late 1990s, although, as previously noted, in the US the term 'learning management system' (LMS) has become more prevalent. The VLE is defined as:

> ... learning management software systems that synthesise the functionality of computer-mediated communications software (e-mail, bulletin boards, newsgroups) and on-line methods of delivering course materials (e.g. the WWW). (Britain and Liber, 1999)

Parallel developments in computer-mediated communication (CMC) and web technology were pivotal in creating what could be regarded as a 'learning environment'. A VLE is a secure course website, with a number of other tools available that allow communication, the creation of online assessments and various other course management functionalities. VLEs have a number of other important features that set them aside from earlier developments, including student management, tracking and monitoring capabilities. These allow students to upload assignments, and tutors to record grades or marks. These systems are also becoming increasingly integrated with student records systems: VLEs integrate these tools in a secure 'one-stop' environment.

Managed learning environments

VLEs are increasingly being seen as 'managed learning environments' (MLEs) and it is important to distinguish between these two concepts. JISC define MLE accordingly:

> The term Managed Learning Environment (MLE) refers to the whole range of information systems and processes of a college or university (including its VLE if it has one) that contribute directly, or indirectly, to learning and the management of that learning.[6]

Recognising the need for research and support in this area, JISC has provided funding for numerous projects.[7] They have also set up a website to provide advice and support to the higher and further education sectors about information systems for teaching and learning.[8] Figure 2.1 shows how MLEs relate to VLEs.

Tools for virtual learning

A brief overview of the major tools offered by most of the commercial and in-house built VLE systems is provided below. Many exist outside the VLE as stand-alone tools, but the key point is that within the VLE these tools are integrated.

Content delivery tools

Content delivery is often the key component of a virtual learning environment. Staff can make lecture notes, presentations and class handouts available to students in one convenient place. The key

Figure 2.1   Becta diagram showing how MLEs relate to VLEs

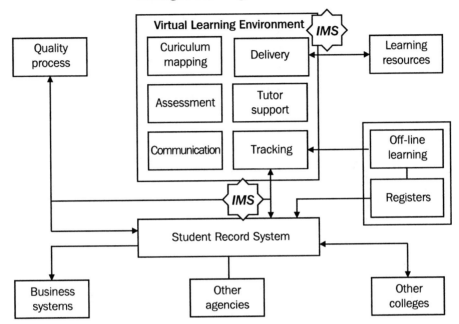

advantage is that the material is secure and only accessible to members of the institution. Most VLE software is relatively easy to use, without specialist knowledge of website creation. Material can be uploaded in a variety of formats.

Communication tools

Most virtual learning environments include communication tools that allow many-to-many interaction, such as bulletin boards or virtual chat rooms. Most VLEs offer facilities to set up discussion groups either for entire classes or for groups of students. These can be used in a variety of ways, but staff often find obvious benefits to answering individual questions in a discussion group which other students can access.

Assessment tools

Online assessment, either for formative or summative purposes, is used in many universities. Self-testing, diagnostic testing or formal assessment can be constructed. Many VLE packages offer such a tool or allow a separate online assessment tool to be plugged in. Multiple-choice questions are relatively easy to construct and have automated marking, which has obvious advantages for large groups of students.

Course management tools

Numerous course management tools are available which enable tutors to record data about student progress or to track individuals or groups of students. Students are able to submit assignments online or have space available to upload presentations or work collaboratively on projects.

Course resources

Many VLEs have course resource areas where tutors can add links to websites or other resources to which they wish to direct students. However, currently these tools are fairly under-developed. The resource area has obvious overlaps with the library, and integration with library systems is increasingly being explored.

Commercial VLE software

Many universities are now using commercial VLE solutions with two clear market leaders in the UK, US and Australia: WebCT (Web Course Tools) and Blackboard. In 2001 a survey by the Teaching, Learning and Information sub-Group (TLIG) of the Universities and Colleges Information Systems Association (UCISA) on the management and implementation of VLEs in UK universities and colleges found that WebCT was the most commonly used VLE. The top four VLEs in order of usage after WebCT were: Blackboard, FirstClass, Lotus LearningSpace and those developed in-house. This study was followed up in 2003 by a complementary survey which found the picture had changed somewhat. Blackboard was by then the most commonly used VLE, with WebCT falling into second place, an intranet-based solution was third and VLEs developed in-house were again fourth.

WebCT was one of the first VLE platforms and it is significant to note that it was developed by and for academics. It was developed in Canada in 1995 by Murray Goldberg, a University of British Columbia computer science professor and launched commercially in 1997. Goldberg created WebCT as an environment to study online learning, and developed the tools to facilitate his research goals while at the same time devising the ability to track appropriate information through the software interface.

In 1999 WebCT merged with Universal Learning Technology (ULT) to become WebCT, Inc. Since this date WebCT has evolved to include numerous options for building the type of teaching and learning environment desired by teaching staff. Additional features include enhanced integration capabilities and security tools.

Meanwhile, WebCT's main rival Blackboard claims to be 'founded with a vision to transform the Internet into a powerful environment for the education experience'.[9] The original teaching and learning software platform was launched in 1997 and known as CourseInfo. The company was formed when two education consultants, Matthew Pittinsky and Michael Chasen, were contracted to help lead the formation of an Educause IMS standards group for online education technology. At the same time, a team at Cornell University was developing an online education software product that would be scalable for wider institutional application. Recognising the high demand for a sophisticated, easy-to-use and affordable online education software platform, the two groups merged to form Blackboard Inc. Blackboard has very similar tools to those available in WebCT.

Current and future e-learning developments

There are a number of developments in e-learning that may change existing tools and how they are used. Increasingly, researchers and practitioners in learning technology are referring to 'learning objects'. These will be discussed in greater detail in Chapter 5. A learning object can take many different forms, but the key feature is reusability, and the construction of metadata to describe the object and its possible use is vital. Increasingly, institutions are being encouraged to set up digital repositories for learning objects.

Next-generation VLEs

The move towards MLEs has been slower than anticipated; however, integrated information systems are undoubtedly the way forward for e-learning. Two developments that may take on great significance are Sakai and the JISC Technical Framework. These two developments have been compared in a recent article on the CETIS website (Kraan, 2004).

Sakai (*http://www.sakaiproject.org/*) describes itself as a community source software development project. It was founded by the University of Michigan, Indiana University, MIT, Stanford, the uPortal Consortium and the Open Knowledge Initiative (OKI) with the support of the Andrew W. Mellon Foundation. The first release for their Collaboration and Learning Environment (CLE) software was in late June 2004. The software is open source and the group is also working with the library community to ensure interoperability. Meanwhile the JISC Technical Framework also aims to create a range of tools using open-source code. Developments will be undertaken through a series of short, focused, community-led projects, which will seek to join up whatever systems the community has or wants to be developed. This has been described as a 'pick 'n' mix' approach to MLE developments. More information is available from JISC about this initiative.[10]

Interoperability and open source initiatives are discussed in more detail in Chapter 5.

E-learning and digital libraries

The overview of e-learning earlier in this chapter and Chapter 1's survey of digital library developments sets the scene for the remainder of this book, which focuses on the integration of these two technologies. Considerable research and development has been undertaken in the UK in particular. Librarians and IT professionals have been increasingly working together since the 1990s as digital technology developed. An example is the many converged library and IT services at universities throughout the world. Furthermore, in 1990 EDUCAUSE and the Association of Research Libraries jointly sponsored the Coalition for Networked Information (CNI). CNI defines itself as:

> ... an organization designed to advance the transformative promise of networked information technology for the improvement of scholarly communication and the enrichment of intellectual productivity.[11]

However, arguably, specific research examining the integration of digital libraries and virtual learning environments began with the UK-based JISC funded INSPIRAL project. This project led to an increased recognition that systems and people need to work together to best serve the needs of the learner.

The INSPIRAL Project

In 2001 JISC funded a six-month project which was to take on enormous significance for the library and e-learning fields. The INSPIRAL (INveStigating Portals for Information Resources and Learning) Project examined the institutional challenges and requirements involved in linking virtual and managed learning environments (VLEs and MLEs) with digital and hybrid libraries. The needs of the learner were paramount to INSPIRAL, and the project focused on UK higher education with an eye to international developments. The ultimate aim of INSPIRAL was to inform JISC's future strategy and funding of initiatives in this area. The project was far sighted in the recognition that the evolution of e-learning and the development of libraries had thus far 'proceed[ed] along different paths' (Currier, 2001) but that their integration would be of enormous benefit to learners. The project focused in particular on organisational problems rather than technical issues. Several deliverables from the project are still highly valuable resources, for example the literature review (Brown and Currier, 2001) and the six case studies of digital library and VLE integration.[12]

Even from its early days, INSPIRAL sparked a large amount of interest and engaged with key stakeholders. An e-mail list was established which still exists today, and in 2001 the project led directly to the launch of the JISC Digital Libraries and Virtual Learning Environments (DiVLE) Programme. INSPIRAL had six major recommendations for the JISC, which covered three main areas: provision of information and guidance, facilitating cooperation and collaboration and funding further research. It was recognised that national guidelines and standards would be essential to further develop VLE and digital library integration, such as metadata specifications, but also staff and user training and education was recognised as important. JISC was asked to provide price guides and real-cost surveys for the implementation of such systems. They also recommended that an independent, comparative guide to specific VLE/MLE and library management systems be established. This would include information on their suitability for linkages and integration, so that institutions were not solely reliant on company information. The recommendations for future research included a study of learner needs, an investigation of developments in Scandinavia and Australia, a look at the non-uptake of e-learning and an investigation of virtual research environments. Finally the JISC was asked to form and support consortia across higher education and further education to facilitate better negotiation with commercial vendors and service providers. Areas where such consortia may have influence were identified as publishers and. publishing culture in general, the vendors of VLE/MLE and library products and sharing resources.

DiVLE Programme overview

By 2001 the benefits to learners of building links between digital libraries and VLEs were clear; however, the practicalities of doing this and the problems it might bring were less so. With this in mind, the JISC DiVLE Programme aimed to explore the technical, pedagogical and organisational issues of linking digital library systems and VLEs.[13] The programme provided:

> ... a vision for an ideal fully integrated online learning environment, which included seamless, one-stop access, all library functions online, and individualisation for the learner, flexibility for the teacher, universal accessibility and ease of use. (JISC, 2001a)

Its specific objectives were to:

- explore the issues of linking VLEs with local institutional digital library resources and services;
- implement curriculum focused pilots, based upon units of learning, linking VLEs to digital library systems;
- provide models and guidelines for other institutions about the cultural and organisational issues related to joining up these systems in an institution.

Nine projects were funded that undertook short practical explorations of linking digital libraries and VLEs and examined the impact on staff, students and the organisation of learning and teaching issues. The tenth project was funded to undertake an overall evaluation and review of the projects in relation to the technical, pedagogical and organisational issues. More information about each project is available on the JISC DiVLE website or on the project's own websites which are listed below; however, the final evaluation project is perhaps of greatest significance and this is examined in some detail. The ten projects funded under this programme included the following.

DELIVER

Digital Electronic Library Integration within Virtual EnviRonments: *http://www.angel.ac.uk/DELIVER*. Hosted jointly at the London School of Economics and De Montfort University, with partnerships from WebCT, Blackboard, Talis and Sirsi, this project was particularly concerned with designing and implementing practical software tools for end-users and administrators of institutional VLEs and library management systems to facilitate the consistent creation and easier use of course-based resource (reading) lists.

DEVIL

Dynamically Enhancing VLE Information from the Library: *http://srv1.mvm.ed.ac.uk/devilweb/index.asp*. The University of Edinburgh was the lead partner in this project along with the Open University and Project Angel. The project examined the means for identifying resources of interest to tutors in creating courses and built on existing work to provide academic staff with tools to permit dynamic data integration between library and other resources and VLE-based courses for a variety of media.

EnCoRe

Enriching Courses with Resources: *http://lib.derby.ac.uk/encore/ encore.html*. EnCoRe was a partnership between librarians and learning technologists at the University of Derby and Openly Informatics. Derby has probably the largest collection of copyright-cleared locally digitised readings in UK higher education to supplement an extensive range of electronic information sources. Meanwhile, the in-house virtual learning environment had almost 500 modules using technology support. Openly Informatics' commercial electronic linking package, 1Cate (one Click Access to everything), was used to further develop and integrate electronic resources within an educational context.

Evaluation of links between VLE and digital libraries in a new medical school

http://www.jisc.ac.uk/index.cfm?Name=project_evalmedi. This project was led by the Peninsula Medical School of Exeter and Plymouth Universities. Its partners included Gold Standard Media, Blackboard and EBSCO. As a new medical school the VLE was to be the primary means of communication with and between students. All core staff at Peninsula Medical School manage their courses through the VLE. The overall aim of the project was to evaluate and assess staff training needs and methods, student needs, training and appreciation of the integrated library and digital environment.

INFORMS

Information Skills Project: *http://informs.hud.ac.uk/cgi-bin/informs.pl*. INFORMS was led by the University of Loughborough and the University of Oxford and built on the previous JISC project INHALE. It recognised that while there had been widespread adoption of VLEs, information skills learning and teaching resources are practically non-existent within them. The project scaled up the INHALE model for delivery of information skills materials to enable the replication, testing and refining of all the models, methodologies, tools and materials already developed by the INHALE project in the area of the delivery of information skills within VLEs.

The 4i project

Linking Library and VLE systems: *http://www.ulster.ac.uk/library/4i*. The University of Ulster worked with WebCT, Talis and Athens on a VLE–library integration pilot. This project continued the work of the successful pilot to accelerate the institutional implementation of integrated VLE and library systems. The aim was to provide users with contextual links and seamless access to appropriate online resources and services. The project assessed the impact of such added value services on users and academic and library business processes. It also developed and tested a more scalable system-independent, interoperable integration methodology.

OLIVE

Open Linking Implementation in a Virtual Learning Environment: *http://www.wmin.ac.uk/olive*. OLIVE was a collaborative project between Royal Holloway, the University of London and the University of Westminster. Partners included Ex Libris, Granada Learning and Blackboard. The project provided a practical exploration of the OpenURL as a method of linking between VLE software and digital library resources at the level of reference lists and learning objects.

PORTOLE

Providing Online Resources to Online Learning Environments: *http://www.leeds.ac.uk/portole/*. This project was led by the University of Leeds, in partnership with the University of Oxford and the Resource Discovery Network. It aimed to produce a range of tools for tutors which enabled them to discover information resources and embed these into their course modules from within a university VLE. PORTOLE produced a set of tools that facilitate the discovery of resources to support an online learning resource, and their embedding into the learning environment.

Talking Systems

http://www.newport.ac.uk/talkingsystems. This project was led by the University of Wales College, Newport, with partners including IBM, Lancaster University, SIRSI and Percussion. It recognised that virtual learning was seeing the emergence of standards for the way online learning materials should be structured. One such standard is the Shareable Content Object Reference Model (SCORM). Talking Systems explored the way that a search and retrieval standard developed by the library community could be used to help universities to share SCORM content they were developing in their VLEs.

LinkER

Linking Digital Libraries and Virtual Learning Environments: Evaluation and Review: *http://www.cerlim.ac.uk/projects/linker/index.php.* Manchester Metropolitan University in partnership with the University of Lancaster provided a formative evaluation of the DiVLE Programme. The main focus of the project was the generic lessons learned from the programme about the integration of digital libraries and VLEs. Evaluation took place by close interaction between the LinkER team and key individuals in each project, mainly through a planned longitudinal series of interviews. Formative feedback was provided to both the individual projects and to JISC.

Evaluation of DiVLE and the findings of LinkER

The DiVLE Programme attracted a considerable amount of attention, running several workshops and establishing an e-mail list. Meanwhile, the LinkER project was invaluable in drawing together the common themes emerging from the nine projects. Three reports were produced by this project in total, including:

- a review of recent developments, achievements and trends in the DiVLE area;
- an interim report on DiVLE emerging issues;
- a final report: the formative evaluation of the DiVLE Programme.

LinkER highlighted that the programme 'gave scope for the exploration of key areas of interest rather than the development of products and services for the community' (Brophy, Markland and Jones, 2003, p. 3). The emerging issues were divided into technological, teaching and learning and organisational. Technological issues concentrated on the lack of consensus for 'library' metadata standards that were applicable to the library and learning community and the need to further test standards such as OpenURL. Cusomisation and interoperability between digital resources and commercial VLEs was also raised as an issue, as was cross searching of resources, access management and the immature development of learning object repositories. These issues are explored in greater detail in Chapter 5.

In teaching and learning issues, LinkER suggested that tools developed by the DiVLE Programme imply considerable changes to the workload and role of academic staff, who may be resistant to such changes without an obvious benefit to themselves or to students. The projects also highlighted that current academic practice in resource selection and reading list construction requires further investigation. Finally the report argued that assumptions could not be made about the willingness of students to engage with VLEs and the digital resources embedded within them. A minority of students were found to have difficulty adapting to the VLE environment, or may be resistant to certain features. Many of these issues are discussed further in Chapter 3, which looks at current and emerging roles for information professionals.

Organisationally, several issues emerged relevant to projects of short duration. LinkER found that several projects had staffing problems. They also recognised that project staff need to be adaptable and flexible. The report emphasised the need for contingency planning before the start of the project to help alleviate the unforeseen risks and when planning a project, staff must consider the alignment of the project timescale with the academic year. This was particularly important when user testing with students or tutors was a key requirement or where a product needs to be rolled out for the start of the next academic year.

LinkER recommended that further work was required, in particular to collate and sythesise the technical work undertaken in the programme. The report also recognised that communication between the projects had been limited and that valuable synergies might have been lost. However, there was some evidence that work from the projects was feeding into international standards. In particular, the work on resource list interoperability led to project members participating in the establishment of an IMS specification in this field. Again these developments are discussed in Chapter 5.

Developments outside the UK

Much of this chapter has concentrated on developments in the UK, which has led much of the research on the integration of digital libraries and VLEs. In the US, government-funded digital library research is largely undertaken by the National Science Foundation (NSF). A recent collaboration with JISC has seen the NSF undertake projects in this area. Additionally, organisations such as OCLC have also launched initiatives which are bringing the wider e-learning and library communities together.

JISC–NSF collaboration: digital libraries in the classroom

Collaboration between the JISC and the NSF started in 1998 with the International Digital Libraries Programme, discussed in Chapter 1. This work continued in 2003 with the launch of the Digital Libraries in the Classroom Programme. The original call for proposals went out in 2001 in line with the increasing recognition that learning technologies and digital library efforts were beginning to converge. The call stated:

> The learning experience is being revolutionised by Information and Communications Technology (ICT) and the Internet in particular. Students increasingly turn to the web for educational and scholarly material. There is a need for better integration of the different technologies and applications being developed in the learning and teaching processes. (JISC, 2001b)

Four projects were funded under this programme, all of which are ongoing and all of which have partner institutions in the UK and the US. The first projects are due to report in 2006.[14] It is difficult to anticipate at this stage what the outcomes might be, but a recent report from McGill (2004), working on the Distributed Innovative Design, Education and Teamworking (DIDET) project at Strathclyde University, suggested that learning technologists and librarians are still culturally distinct. Nevertheless, the experience of bringing together the two communities in an international programme must be an important step towards closer integration.

IMS Global Learning Consortium

IMS came into existence in 1997 as a project within the National Learning Infrastructure Initiative of EDUCAUSE. IMS is a worldwide non-profit organisation that includes more than 50 members, coming from all sectors of the e-learning community, including hardware and software vendors, educational institutions, publishers, government agencies, systems integrators, multimedia content providers and other consortia. The IMS Global Learning Consortium develops and promotes the adoption of open technical specifications for interoperable learning technology. Several IMS specifications have become worldwide standards for delivering learning products and services. IMS specifications and related publications are made available to the public at no charge from the IMS website. No fee is required to implement the specifications.

Specifications are the core of work for IMS, and they have produced specifications for all aspects of e-learning products. Most recently IMS have formed a Digital Libraries Special Interest Group, in recognition of the need to reach out and work with the library community.

OCLC E-learning Taskforce

Librarians will be familiar with OCLC, the Online Computer Library Center, which has over 45,000 member libraries throughout the world. The organisation is dedicated to furthering access to the world's information and reducing information costs. In recognition of the growing importance of e-learning to libraries, an OCLC e-Learning Taskforce was set up in early 2003. The Taskforce's key aim is to:

> Assist OCLC in defining strategies and services that both help libraries deliver services in this arena and help the academic community leverage library services within elearning. (OCLC, 2003)

A background paper for the Taskforce appeared in March 2003, written by Neil McLean (McLean, 2003) from IMS Australia, with a view to identifying the main organisational and technical issues facing institutions that were moving towards online learning environments. McLean identified digital asset management as being an issue of crucial importance for an institution. Digital assets were defined as the range of digital information and learning activities and included a wealth of material such as learning objects, digital library collections, commercially licensed information services and research publications. The paper identified several types of systems, such as content management systems, virtual learning environments and integrated library management systems, which are currently all competing for supremacy. However, arguably none currently provide a total solution for digital asset management.

In October 2003 OCLC produced its White Paper, focusing on concrete strategies for libraries and for OCLC as a library cooperative (OCLC, 2003). Under the title *Libraries and the Enhancement of E-learning*, the relationship between academic libraries and e-learning is explored. It is aimed at the library community but also more widely at the global academic community. The paper made recommendations that OCLC, as a library advocate, should assist libraries in raising awareness among the academic community and commercial vendors of the benefits of library involvement in virtual learning environments. They should also promote the idea of service convergence to provide learners with improved access. The Taskforce also recommended that OCLC should integrate learning object management support into their products and services.

Conclusion

This chapter has examined several definitions of e-learning, how it developed and a brief overview of the tools that are currently available. More importantly it has looked at the increasing body of research that suggests that e-learning is highly relevant to librarians. In particular, the publication of the OCLC E-learning Taskforce White Paper signifies wide recognition among the global library profession that e-learning is having a major impact on their work. In the UK, through the work of JISC, librarians have now been involved in learning technology projects for a number of years. Two professions and two cultures are finding their future increasingly aligned. While two separate roles will remain, organisations are increasingly recruiting individuals with knowledge of both areas. The remainder of this book goes on to discuss some of the key topics that librarians will need to understand to be fully engaged with digital library and e-learning developments.

Notes

1. See: *http://www.ed.gov/about/offices/list/os/technology/index.html*

2. See: *http://www.ed.gov/pubs/edtechprograms/theexpertpanel.pdf.*

3. See: *http://www.educause.edu/*

4. See: *http://www.alt.ac.uk/sigs.html*

5. See: HEFCE Report 99/39. Use of TLTP materials in UK higher education. Available from: *http://www.hefce.ac.uk/pubs/hefce/1999/99_39.htm*

6. See: *http://www.jisc.ac.uk/index.cfm?name=mle_overview*

7. See: *http://www.jisc.ac.uk/index.cfm?name=mle_programmes*

8. See: *http://www.jiscinfonet.ac.uk/*

9. More information is available: *http://www.blackboard.com/about/index.htm*

10. See: *http://www.jisc.ac.uk/funding_elearning_demos.html*

11. See: *http://www.cni.org/organization.html*

12. See: *http://inspiral.cdlr.strath.ac.uk/documents/casestudies.html*

13. Linking Digital Libraries with VLEs (DiVLE) Programme website. *http://www.jisc.ac.uk/index.cfm?name=programme_divle*

14. More information is available on the JISC website: *http://www.jisc.ac.uk/index.cfm?name=programme_dlitc*

References

Appelmans, Thomas (2002) *E-learning.* Available from: *http://student.vub.ac.be/~tappelma/communicatie/e-learning.pdf.*

Britain, Sandy and Liber, Oleg (1999) *A framework for pedagogical evaluation of virtual learning environments*, JTAP report. Available from: *http://www.jtap.ac.uk/reports/htm/jtap-041.html.*

Brophy, P., Markland, M. and Jones, C. (2003) *Link[ER]: Linking Digital Libraries and Virtual Learning Environments: Evaluation and Review Final Report: Formative Evaluation of the DiVLE Programme.* Deliverable D5, Link[ER] Project, Centre for Research in Library and Information Management.

Brown, S. and Currier, S. (2001) *INSPIRAL Project Literature Review.* Available from: *http://inspiral.cdlr.strath.ac.uk/documents/litrev.pdf.*

Conole, G. and Oliver, M. (2002) 'Embedding theory into learning technology practice with toolkits', *Journal of Interactive Media in Education*, 8. Available from: *www-jime.open.ac.uk/2002/8.*

Currier, Sarah (2001) 'INSPIRAL: digital libraries and virtual learning environments', *Ariadne*, 22 June, 28. Available from: *http://www.ariadne.ac.uk/issue28/inspiral/intro.html*.

Dede, Christopher (1990) 'The evolution of distance learning: technology-mediated interactive learning', *Journal of Research on Computing in Education*, 22(1): 247–65.

Department for Education and Skills (DfES) (2003) *Towards a Unified e-Learning Strategy*, Consultation Document. Available from: *http://www.dfes.gov.uk/consultations2/16/docs/towards%20a%20unified%20e-learning%20strategy.pdf*.

Gibbs, G. (2001) *Analysis of strategies for learning and teaching*, HEFCE Report 01/37a. Available from: *http://www.hefce.ac.uk/Pubs/hefce/2001/01_37a.htm*.

HEFCE (1999) *Communications and information technology materials for learning and teaching in UK higher and further education*, HEFCE Report Ref 99/60a, October. Available from: *http://www.hefce.ac.uk/Pubs/099_60a.zip*.

JISC (2001a) Linking Digital Libraries with VLEs (DiVLE) Programme home page. Available from: *http://www.jisc.ac.uk/index.cfm?name=programme_divle*.

JISC (2001b) *Digital libraries and the classroom*, Circular 7/01. Available from: *http://www.jisc.ac.uk/index.cfm?name=circular_7_01*.

Kraan, W. (2004) *Same area, different goals; Sakai and the JISC framework programme*. CETIS website. Available from: *http://www.cetis.ac.uk/content2/20040503155445*.

Laurillard, D. (1979) 'The process of student learning', *Higher Education*, 8: 395–409.

Laurillard, D. (1991) 'Mediating the message: television programme design and students' understanding', *Instructional Science*, 20: 3–23.

Laurillard, D. (1993) *Rethinking University Teaching: A Conversational Framework for the Effective Use of Educational Technologies*. London: Routledge.

Laurillard, D. (2002) *Rethinking University Teaching: A Conversational Framework for the Effective Use of Learning Technologies*, 2nd edn. London: Routledge.

McLean, N. (2003) *Managing online learning and information environments*, OCLC E-learning Taskforce, Background paper. Available from: *http://www.oclc.org/community/topics/elearning/groups/taskforce/background/default.htm*.

Mcgill, L. (2004) *Lost in Translation: trying to decipher the differing perceptions of information, and other, e-literacy's held by various in*

Higher Education institutions [*sic*], paper given at Elit2004. Abstract available from: *http://www.elit-conf.org/elit2004/docs/sess5rma3 .html.*

National Committee of Inquiry into Higher Education (NCIHE) in the Learning Society (1997) *Higher Education in the Learning Society (Dearing Report).* London: HMSO/NCIHE.

OCLC (2003) *Libraries and the enhancement of e-learning,* OCLC E-learning Taskforce White Paper. Available from: *http://www.oclc.org/ community/topics/elearning/groups/taskforce/default.htm.*

Oliver, M. (2000) *What's the Purpose of Theory in Learning Technology?* Positional Paper at the Learning Technology Theory Workshop, ALT-C 2000, Manchester.

Salmon, G. (2002) *E-Moderating: The Key to Teaching and Learning Online.* London: Kogan Page.

E-learning and information literacy

Introduction

We have seen in Chapter 2 how the development of e-learning is changing education: in many ways making learning more flexible and more tailored to individual needs. This chapter discusses how developments in information literacy are taking place alongside the development of e-learning to change the role of librarians and information professionals. However, the chapter also explains how libraries have always been an integral part of learning, helping learners find, evaluate and exploit resources. Yet now, with an increasing number of digital resources, librarians have a crucial role in navigating learners through the complex digital information environment. Librarians have been teaching students for many years, for example through library induction sessions or hands-on training in the use of library databases. This chapter argues that librarians need to move away from this more traditional approach to training, towards developing integrated information literacy programmes. They need to work alongside teaching staff to demonstrate their specific expertise, and build programmes that are integrated into the curriculum.

This chapter provides an overview of recent developments and research within the learning support and information literacy field. It provides practical examples of initiatives that librarians can become involved in. The wider concept of 'e-literacy' is discussed to identify the skills that both learners and teachers require to fully exploit e-learning. Information literacy initiatives in the UK are somewhat behind the US and Australia in achieving widespread recognition for librarians as educators and raising the profile of information literacy. Developments from these two countries are therefore particularly useful. However, Chapter 2 has suggested that for integrated library and e-learning solutions, developments in the UK are very much leading the way. By combining the information literacy expertise from the US and Australia with e-learning solutions and the growing recognition of the need for e-literacy in the UK, the chapter identifies a clear role for librarians in the future.

The new professionals

There can be no doubt that the library profession has changed enormously in the last 5–10 years. While the profession has always been evolving, adapting to new technologies, new media and the ever-changing needs of users, more recently these changes have accelerated to match rapid developments in information and communication technologies. The Internet has dramatically increased the range of information available and the way in which it is delivered. It is hardly believable that the first web browser technology was only invented ten years ago. Similarly, e-mail, something taken for granted by many today, was unknown outside of higher education as little as ten years ago. Library students in the early 1990s were taught about developments such as 'Gophers' and used telnet connections to connect to other universities' online catalogues. Such technologies seem primitive and outdated today since the rise of the World Wide Web and broadband connectivity. It is difficult to imagine what developments the future will bring; nevertheless, the library profession will need to embrace these changes and move with the times to meet the needs of users.

As the technology changes, so the skills that librarians need as professionals must evolve. Information and communication technologies have changed the expectations and demands of library users and the skills and training that the users need has also evolved. In higher education particularly, but also across the sectors, librarians are increasingly seen as being part of a wider group of learning support staff, which includes IT specialists, learning technologists, web editors and other staff. During the 1990s many libraries went through convergence with IT departments; however, we are now starting to see the development of truly hybrid teams. This chapter urges librarians to recognise their role as crucial players in this growing profession of learning support staff, working in partnership with learning technologists, instructional designers, IT staff and education staff. Not only does this mean librarians need to work with new groups of people, but they need to be clear about the unique and highly relevant skills that they can offer. Our ability to teach information or e-literacy skills to learners and teachers alike must surely ensure our central role in the education sector. Moreover, traditional skills such as cataloguing and classification are highly transferable into the e-environment, where the creation of high-quality metadata is crucial to the success of digital repositories. These more technical considerations are discussed in more detail in Chapter 5.

Information literacy and the 'access paradox'

Information literacy has its roots in library user education, whereby librarians inducted new users to the services offered by the library and taught them something about finding and evaluating information. With the rise of the Internet and web technology there can be no doubting that access to information has improved. Nevertheless, to assume that because information is available on the Web, people will have the skills and knowledge to find, access and use it effectively is naive. As Diana Laurillard says:

> It is as absurd to try and solve the problems of education by giving people access to information as it would be to solve the housing problem by giving people access to bricks. (Quoted in Big Blue, 2001)

Staff often assume that students entering higher education have well-developed information literacy skills; however, there is considerable evidence to suggest that their use of the Internet is at best 'haphazard'. The JISC-funded JUSTEIS project reported in 2000:

> There is no doubting the effect of the Internet on information seeking by staff and students at all institutions; search engines and known sites are the first resort for most academic queries, as well as for many personal domestic queries ... Given the wide range of engines used and the haphazard nature of much of the searching, some thought might be given to ways of encouraging students to use the Internet more effectively. (Armstrong et al., 2000)

The increasing amount of information available on the Internet has given rise to what has been called by some librarians as 'the Google generation'. Students are frequently using the popular search engine Google as their first port of call when searching for all types of information on the Internet, rather than using subscription databases and quality information resources. There are countless examples from librarians throughout the world who are battling to counter this belief that everything can be found through one search engine. Gibbons (2003) recently published a rallying cry to librarians maintaining:

> ... with increasing frequency in a world where information is rapidly becoming both digitized and personalized, the relevancy of libraries is being questioned. (Gibbons, 2003, p. 1)

Gibbons goes on to argue how '... patrons arrive at the library website with expectations raised through the personalized use of My Yahoo pages ...' The wider aim of the paper argues the case for the continuing existence of libraries and their relevance in the digital age. Scare statistics are presented such as '73% of college students [are] using the Internet instead of the library as their primary site for information searches'.

Information literacy skills are particularly important now with the increasing wealth of electronic resources currently available. Borah et al. (2004) characterise this as the 'access paradox' where an increasing amount of information exists in electronic format but users are less able to find what they need because they don't have sufficient skills. There is a real challenge in equipping learners with the skills they need to function in the electronic environment. Information literacy is just one of these skills, but librarians have an important role in helping learners find quality resources in whatever format they exist. In the UK the primary motivation for the establishment of the subject-based gateways, which collectively make up the Resource Discovery Network (RDN), was to provide a portal for quality Internet resources. However, evidence suggests that subject gateways are another of the under-exploited tools created by librarians – with users preferring the ease and speed of Google. Reporting again from the JUSTEIS project, Thomas (2004) tells how library websites and tools developed by librarians are under-used by students across further and higher education. Librarians need to consider the motivations of their users and make information literacy both timely and relevant to learners.

Definitions of information literacy

It is useful to first define information literacy for the purposes of this chapter. The concept has been defined in numerous ways by authors in the field, but it is generally understood to include the following skills:

- knowledge of information resources in one's subject;
- the ability to construct effective search strategies;
- the ability to critically appraise information sources;
- the ability to use information sources appropriately, and to cite and create references.

Webber and Johnson (2000) recognise that definitions of information literacy vary but generally include the following knowledge and skills:

- effective information seeking;
- informed choice of information sources;
- information evaluation and selection;
- comfort in using a range of media to best advantage;
- awareness of issues to do with bias and reliability of information; and
- effectiveness in transmitting information to others.

In the UK the term 'information skills' is still used in many institutions; however, Bruce (1997), writing her thesis on the seven faces of information literacy, argued that information literacy should not be regarded as skills and training, but as seven stages to becoming information literate. She maintained that:

> Information literacy is about people's ability to operate effectively in an information society. This involves critical thinking, an awareness of personal and professional ethics, information evaluation, conceptualising information needs, organising information, interacting with information professionals and making effective use of information in problem-solving, decision-making and research. It is these information based processes which are crucial to the character of learning organisations and which need to be supported by the organisation's technology infrastructure. (Bruce, 1997)

An even broader term that is starting to enter the literature is 'e-literacy', which has been defined as the converging of IT literacy and information literacy. It been closely linked to e-learning and has been the subject of an international conference since 2002.[1] The conference describes e-literacy as: 'a crucial enabler of individuals and institutions in moving successfully in a world reliant upon electronic tools and facilities'.

Martin (2003) describes how e-literacy encompasses aspects of computer literacy, information literacy, thinking and learning skills, and what he terms media and moral literacy. He argues that:

> E-literacy is gradually coming to be seen as a challenge which educators, and those who shape education, must address as a priority. At the least, it means avoiding the inequalities wrought by differential access to e-facilities; at the most, it means enabling everybody to make their way with confidence in the e-world.

Information literacy standards

In many aspects of information literacy education, the US and Australia are both more advanced than the UK, in particular with established information literacy standards. They both also have greater standardisation in the delivery of information literacy programmes and with information literacy being incorporated into the curriculum at all education levels. In the UK, while information skills feature within the National Curriculum for pre-16 education, within the further and higher education sectors a strategic approach to information skills training for students is yet to be established, although a JISC-funded project, the Big Blue, went some way towards achieving this.

US and Australian information literacy standards

In 1998 the Association of College and Research Libraries (ACRL) in the USA established a Task Force on Information Literacy Competency Standards and charged it to develop competency standards in this area for higher education. In 2000 the group published its *Information Literacy Competency Standards for Higher Education* (ACRL, 2000). The full text of the standards is available on their website, together with a number of case studies of how the standards are being used. The ACRL recognises the central role of information literacy for developing lifelong learners. Five broad standards were established, each with performance indicators and specific outcomes. These included:

1. The information-literate student determines the nature and extent of the information needed.

2. The information-literate student accesses needed information effectively and efficiently.

3. The information-literate student evaluates information and its sources critically and incorporates selected information into his or her knowledge base and value system.

4. The information-literate student, individually or as a member of a group, uses information effectively to accomplish a specific purpose.

5. The information-literate student understands many of the economic, legal and social issues surrounding the use of information and accesses and uses information ethically and legally.

The standards provide a framework for assessing the information literate individual. The established competencies can be used as indicators of information literacy by academic staff and librarians.

Meanwhile, following the work of the ACRL, the Council of Australian University Librarians published its Information Literacy Standards (CAUL, 2001). They reviewed the US standards published the previous year and added two additional standards of their own: a new Standard 6 which addresses the ability of an individual to control and manipulate information, and Standard 7 that represents information literacy as the intellectual framework, providing the potential for lifelong learning.

UK information literacy developments

In the UK, SCONUL (Society of College, National and University Libraries) acknowledged the need to address the issue of information literacy and information skills training for students with the formation of the SCONUL Information Skills Task Force in December 1998. The SCONUL Task Force in their paper *Information skills in higher education: a SCONUL position paper* (SCONUL, 1999) went some way toward achieving this and highlighted a number of issues which have formed the basis for further evaluation. The Task Force has identified two levels of competency to the acquisition of information skills within higher education. The first relates to study skills, or the tools needed to be a learner, which students will require to undertake a course of study. This includes:

■ the ability to use a library and its resources;

■ the ability to search for literature;

■ appropriate use of citations and references.

SCONUL also developed what are known as the Seven Pillars of Information Literacy (see Figure 3.1), which have been used by a number of UK universities, notably the University of Sheffield and University of Leeds, to develop an information literacy programme.

Figure 3.1   **SCONUL's Seven Pillars of Information Literacy**

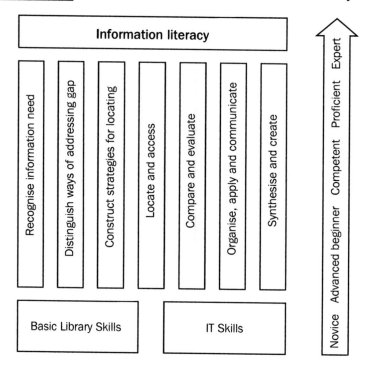

Consequently, partly in recognition of the need for further work in this area, JISC funded the Big Blue Project in 2001 (Big Blue, 2001).[2] The project examined the position of information skills in the post-16 education sector in the UK from a variety of perspectives identifying, wherever possible, examples of good practice. The project made a number of recommendations, including the following:

- JISC in conjunction with bodies such as SCONUL and the Chartered Institute of Library and Information Professionals (CILIP) should form a national forum for information skills to encourage institutions to share experiences and promote the area.

- Assessments should be carried out to examine the baseline skills of students and how these improve over time following information skills training and the application of these skills to their academic work.

- Further work to investigate the level of information skills among academic staff should be undertaken.

- Further work into the establishment of standards and performance indicators in information skills should be carried out, drawing in particular on the US and Australian work in this area.

Moreover, the project recognised that one of the biggest problems in UK further and higher education institutions is convincing those outside of the library of the importance of information literacy and ensuring it is integrated into the curriculum. There are also problems in tying formal assessments to information literacy programmes, which means that students are less likely to take the courses seriously.

SCONUL are an important lobbying group for librarians and in 2003 they published a briefing paper entitled *Information support for eLearning: principles and practices* (SCONUL, 2003). The paper's intended audience was primarily partners in the UK e-University initiative, which was set up in 2001 to deliver online courses throughout the world.[3] However, the paper recognised that the principles and delivery mechanisms 'are relevant to anyone with an interest in efficient eLearning' (SCONUL, 2003, p. 2). SCONUL recognises the important role for librarians in developing efficient e-learning and those considering e-learning ventures are urged to talk to library and information professionals about course support. Information literacy is a central principle of the briefing paper, which states:

> All eLearners must be given the opportunity to develop and enhance their skills in finding and using information. This not only ensures that they can fully exploit information resources for their eLearning course, but also provides them with a life skill. (SCONUL, 2003, p. 5)

The paper discusses the importance of integration between the delivery of course materials and information support. It also provides a good example of how librarians need to promote their skills to the wider education community. This is discussed in more detail later in this chapter. However, promoting information literacy to academic staff still remains a challenge that many librarians must face.

E-literacy and e-learning

Many librarians will be familiar with the term 'information literacy' but e-literacy is a relatively new term emanating from the Universities of Glasgow, Glasgow Caledonian and Strathclyde in Scotland. Martin (2003) argues that:

> The notion of e-literacy is based on the assumption that there are skills, awarenesses and understandings which will enable individuals firstly to survive and secondly to be more effective in their e-encounters.

He goes on to define e-literacy as being comprised of computer, information, media, moral and media literacy. The Elit conference attracts IT support providers, librarians, educationists, educators, researchers and policy-makers. In many ways these e-literacy skills are more relevant to librarians involved in e-learning initiatives than simply considering information literacy in isolation. However, the field is less well established and the terminology less well defined, so introducing the concept to academic staff is not without problems. However, one of the advantages the term e-literacy has over information literacy is the use of the letter 'e'. Just as e-learning as a concept has very quickly fallen into mainstream use, so perhaps e-literacy will give librarians the edge when selling their skills?

E-literacy/information literacy for academic staff

Much of the work on information literacy has concentrated on skills and education for students or learners; however, a crucial area must be the information literacy levels of staff who are responsible for the development and implementation of e-learning. Following on from the Big Blue Project, JISC funded the six-month Big Blue Connect Project (Big Blue Connect, 2003).[4] This project carried out a survey of academic, managerial, administrative and technical staff to establish how staff access and use information within their work environment. The research found there was a general lack of staff awareness about information skills and a lack of training for staff, in particular non-teaching staff. Where training existed it focused primarily on the development of ICT skills and if staff had received training in the development of information skills, it was mainly in the form of a one-off training session to support the introduction of a new service or resource.

Developing information literacy skills, or e-literacy skills, is essential for academic and other support staff to be able to fully engage and exploit library resources in the e-learning system. Engaging with academic staff to develop their own skills also makes them more likely to see the value of building these skills into their courses for students. Building on information literacy programmes offered to students, library staff will need to play an important role in delivering this type of e-literacy education to other staff members. E-literacy skills for staff might include knowledge of the range of resources available in the digital library, such as which journal titles are available in electronic format. But it would also include teaching a member of staff to build an online reading list and add stable links to electronic journal articles. E-literacy also involves knowledge about copyright and licensing arrangements for electronic resources, what Martin (2003) terms moral issues. So staff would receive guidance and support about issues such as which resources are licensed to allow downloading for use in the virtual learning environment and which must be linked to. Copyright and licensing is discussed in greater detail in Chapter 4. Nevertheless, library staff will increasingly be called upon to offer guidance in this area through a variety of means such as:

- one-to-one training and support for guidance on specific issues;
- group training sessions for more routine problems such as setting up an online reading list or learning to use the digital library;
- documentation (printed and web based) that staff can consult on a need-to-know basis.

It is important that e-literacy programmes are not exclusively designed for academic staff or those at the front line in the delivery of e-learning. Library staff should recognise that there is often a team of people who are involved in any e-learning project. Administrative staff, such as departmental or faculty managers and secretaries, are often responsible for updating the information within the virtual learning environment. Tasks such as setting up online reading lists may also be routinely undertaken by administrative staff. It is important that the training is offered as widely as possible and is available to other learning support staff.

Librarians as teachers

In the past, few graduates entering into the library and information profession would say immediately that they were drawn to librarianship to teach. Yet teaching is something that many librarians routinely undertake, through a variety of means. As computers became widespread throughout organisations, increasingly librarians have needed to teach using computers. This started out as teaching users skills such as searching the online library catalogue; however, it very soon extended to teaching users to search online databases, formulate Internet search strategies and use a variety of subject specific databases and electronic resources. As we have seen earlier in this chapter, the widespread development of information literacy programmes means that teaching is something many librarians now undertake routinely.

The curriculum of library schools has undoubtedly changed dramatically in the last ten years as a consequence of developments in ICTs. However, it is not clear if newly qualified librarians are graduating with the full set of skills they require to teach. As well as information literacy theories and principles, librarians increasingly need practical skills to be able to teach. Similarly, topics such as learning theories, pedagogy and e-learning are yet to be incorporated into many library school curricula. It is noteworthy that one topic that has been added to many curricula at library schools is research methods. It has been increasingly recognised that a significant amount of library and information work is project based and there is an obvious need to ensure the profession is equipped with the appropriate research skills. Over the last ten years there has been an enormous amount of public money made available for library research from bodies such as JISC in the UK and the NSF in the US. In the UK, money has been made available to public libraries under initiatives such as the New Opportunities Fund (NOF) and to academic libraries as part of the Research Support Libraries Programme (RSLP).

However, the role of librarians as educators, teaching information literacy skills, either face to face or on the Internet or through a virtual learning environment, has witnessed an enormous growth in the last ten years. It is imperative that library schools provide their graduates with the appropriate skills to carry out this type of work. In part this seems to reflect the tradition in many UK universities of focusing on research in preference to teaching. Therefore the ability of a library to attract research funding for a project is more highly valued than the ability of a library to provide appropriate and timely information literacy education.

Another important issue is the need to embed information literacy skills into the curriculum as early as possible. The lack of professional librarians in many primary and secondary schools is a key problem. One way of tackling this is for teachers to recognise the important role of the librarian. Therefore, Secker and Price (2004) argue that information literacy needs to be an important part of the education of trainee teachers, and that teachers must be encouraged to work with librarians. While we are not advocating that teachers become librarians or vice versa, partnerships between these professions must be strengthened. Currently it seems that learning how to teach is a skill many librarians learn on the job or through their continuing professional development. The next section considers how those within the profession can obtain the skills they require.

The need for continuing professional development

Continuing professional development has always been important in the library profession, with numerous training courses and conferences in which practitioners and researchers can share experiences and learn new skills. In the UK, US and Australia the professional bodies supporting librarians and information professionals all play an important role in continuing professional development. In the UK, a group of librarians have recently set up an Information Literacy sub-group of the Chartered Institute of Library and Information Professionals (CILIP), with a cross-sector remit. Similarly the American Libraries Association (ALA) has an AASL/ACRL Interdivisional Committee on Information Literacy. Groups such as these allow librarians working on information literacy to build networks of support and enable them to share experiences.

Professional bodies increasingly offer training events and conferences that ensure staff are able to develop their knowledge and learn new skills as their jobs evolve. Information literacy has been the theme of several recent meetings and conferences of groups such as the Association of College and Research Libraries in the US. However, more informal networks facilitated by technology are also important. E-mail lists are an extremely useful way of keeping up to date: for example the JISCmail Information Literacy mailing list, which was established in 1998, has over 800 members.[5] More recently, one of the best ways of keeping up to date is through the Information Literacy Weblog, established by lecturers at the University of Sheffield (Webber, Johnston and Boon, 2004) in April 2003. Notices of events, conferences and publications of relevance to the field are regularly posted on the site. Rather than an e-mail list that sends messages to all the group, a weblog (or blog) is rather like an online notice-board, although it has other features, allowing members to post comments and receive notifications of new messages. These less formal means of networking are at least as important as more formal education opportunities discussed subsequently.

Educational opportunities for librarians

In 1999 JISC funded an eLib Project, EduLib, specifically to enhance educational expertise and teaching skills in the higher education library and information services community. The project ran a series of workshops which were attended by over 250 participants. However, it still remains difficult for librarians in post-16 colleges to gain recognition for their role as teaching staff and for academic staff to see them as equal partners. Some have attributed this attitude to the emphasis in librarianship on 'training' rather than teaching that tends to dominate information literacy education. Many information literacy programmes also tend to focus on specific tools and databases rather than teaching principles and the underlying theories. One way to shift this emphasis is to ensure librarians are involved in the development of all new courses from the outset. Where possible, information literacy should be embedded into the curriculum, and delivered jointly by faculty members and library staff.

Netskills is one avenue open to UK librarians offering wider training opportunities.[6] It was established by JISC in 1995 to provide quality Internet training for UK higher education. Their remit has since been extended to offer training to further education but also to the commercial and non-commercial sector. Broadly their services fall into three categories, including: delivering workshops at regional centres throughout the UK or on-site, developing training materials for use by other trainers available under licence and the provision of online, self-paced tutorials. Courses cover a range of topics, but they are frequently attended by librarians and other learning support staff. Recently, Netskills have been offering several different courses covering topics related to e-learning.

Librarians might also consider gaining formal qualifications in education or learning technology. Numerous accredited courses are available, with an increasing number of postgraduate qualifications in learning technology and e-learning. Oliver et al. (2004, p. 49) provides a useful indication of the range of e-learning courses available for learning technologists in UK higher education. If academic librarians are specifically interested in gaining recognition for their skills as teachers then accreditation by the Institute of Learning and Teaching for Higher Education (ILTHE) is the most obvious route. The scheme is primarily aimed at academic staff, but increasing numbers of librarians have been accredited in this way. This route is discussed in more detail below.

Extending your network

Networking between librarians has always been well established, with high levels of participation. However, arguably librarians now need to consider extending their network beyond the library profession and becoming involved in other external groups. A danger is that if librarians continue to network and talk only with others in the profession they will become marginalised, instead of playing a central role in the learning support field. A number of relevant organisations and bodies are listed below, with details of their websites. To be taken seriously as learning support professionals, librarians need to build connections with other groups of professionals and ensure they have representation in other groups. Many of these groups are UK-based, but librarians outside the UK are urged to seek similar bodies in their own countries.

Higher Education Academy

The Higher Education Academy incorporates the Institute of Learning and Teaching (*www.heacademy.ac.uk/*). In the UK the Institute for Learning and Teaching for Higher Education (ILTHE), mentioned above, was formed to recognise expertise in teaching and learning. Specifically it aimed to:

- improve teaching and learning and the quality of the student experience in higher education;
- provide a focus for professional development in teaching and learning of staff in higher education;
- raise the status of, and enhance the respect for, teaching and the support of learning in higher education.

Membership of the ILTHE was open to librarians who could be formally accredited through undertaking the programme. There was also an active ILT Librarians' Forum which met to discuss a number of issues, with information literacy very much at its heart. By achieving ILT accreditation, some in the library profession felt that librarians would be taken more seriously as teachers.

In May 2004 the ILTHE announced it would become part of the Higher Education Academy.[7] The Academy will be formally launched in Autumn 2004 and its remit will be wider than the ILTHE as it will also incorporate the Learning and Teaching Support Network (LTSN). The Higher Education Academy will have a number of roles, including advising on policies and practices that impact on the student experience, supporting curriculum and pedagogic development and facilitating development of and increasing the professional standing of all staff in higher education. All current members of the ILTHE will transfer into the new HE Academy during the summer of 2004 as a list of accredited practitioners and will be the first professionals in the country to be recognised as such. It will be important for librarians to have a role in the Academy and that the Librarians' Forum continues.

The Learning and Teaching Support Network (LTSN) was funded by the four higher education funding bodies in England, Scotland, Wales and Northern Ireland; however, they have now been incorporated into the Academy. They were set up to promote high-quality learning and teaching in higher education through the development and transfer of good practices in all disciplines. The network consisted of 24 subject centres based in higher education institutions throughout the UK and a single generic centre. The LTSN aimed to shape the thinking of policy-makers and provide higher education communities with a stronger voice in national debates and discussions. Subject librarians were often involved in their respective subject centre. Support for the library profession was also provided through the LTSN for Information and Computer Sciences. Furthermore, in 2002 several subject centres collaborated to host a Librarian's Day which examined a range of issues related to teaching and learning. The valuable contribution of librarians needs to be maintained as this organisation becomes part of a wider group.

Association for Learning Technology

The Association for Learning Technology (ALT: *www.alt.ac.uk/*) is a UK-based professional and scholarly association which brings together those with an interest in the use of learning technology. ALT aims specifically to:

- promote good practice in the use of learning technologies in education and industry;
- represent the members in areas of policy;
- facilitate collaboration between practitioners, researchers and policy-makers.[8]

The Association was formed in 1994 and is celebrating its ten-year anniversary in 2004. It publishes a newsletter and a quarterly peer-reviewed journal. It also organises the main academic conference for UK learning technologists. A number of librarians have attended this conference, and in 2003, following the launch of the DiVLE Programme, some integration between the communities took place. The Association is currently working towards establishing an accreditation framework.

Oliver (2004) provides an overview of professional bodies for learning technologists from around the world and finds that in Australia and New Zealand there is no corresponding body. In the United States he cites similarities between the role of instructional technologists and learning technologists. Meanwhile in Europe several organisations are identified, including:

- the European Institute for E-Learning (EIfEL);
- the European Distance Education Network (EDEN);
- the European Federation for Open and Distance Learning (EFODL);
- the European Association for Distance Learning (EADL).

UCISA

UCISA (Universities and Colleges Information Systems Association: *http://www.ucisa.ac.uk/*) is not an organisation that librarians have traditionally been associated with, as its focus is very much information systems. However, UCISA has a number of sub-groups, including the Teaching, Learning and Information Group (TLIG). This group organises conferences and training events which may include areas of mutual interest for librarians.[9] Moreover, UCISA has increasingly been working more closely with SCONUL and in January 2004 organised a joint event. Entitled 'e-learning: the evolving role of academic services', the event was organised in recognition of the mutual interest in the subject.[10] It also highlighted the increasing overlap between the roles of library and learning technology staff. The event sought to bring together the two communities to hear from those working with these issues, and to provide a forum to share and debate them among delegates. It is anticipated that similar events will be held in the future and librarians should be encouraged to attend.

Practical approaches

This chapter concludes with a summary of a number of practical ways that librarians can become involved in e-learning through information literacy programmes and the development of online tutorials. Further information, in the form of detailed case studies, to support this chapter is presented in Chapter 6.

Developing online tutorials

One of the most common initiatives being developed by librarians are self-paced online tutorials available from the library website. These are designed to allow students to learn topics as and when they require the knowledge at a time and place convenient to them. However, a major criticism of these packages is that they can be badly designed and structured, with few interactive features which engage the learner. It is often difficult to obtain feedback.

To develop these packages, there is a range of skills the librarian must learn, or they must acquire from an educational technologist or web designer. If you are planning to develop an online tutorial, it is essential that you consider the following:

- Do you have knowledge of web-authoring and web design or do you have access to someone with these skills?
- Do you have knowledge of pedagogy and how to teach online, or access to someone who does?
- How will you engage the learner and develop interactivity into the package?
- Will there be some form of assessment in the package? Or how will the learner be able to check their progress?
- How will you monitor usage of the package and evaluate its benefits?

Advantages of web-based tutorials

Materials made available from the library website can be used by any library user. They are particularly valuable for generic sessions, such as a virtual tour of the library, where library visitors as well as members of the institution may wish to use the tutorial. You may consider making the package available on the Web but password protecting it, or making it available via an intranet so that only authorised users – in the case of a university this would be registered students and staff – can access it.

Disadvantages of web-based tutorials

Web-based tutorials are not without problems, in particular:

- they need a lot of work to develop, and to update, particularly if produced using flat HTML pages – consider using a VLE or a content management system for ease of updating;
- they often require detailed knowledge of web design or educational technology to set up;
- it can be difficult to make them interactive.

Using the virtual learning environment

An alternative to making information literacy materials available on the Web is to use the virtual learning environment software. Materials can be embedded into existing subject-based courses or a separate information literacy module can be made available to students. The advantages of using the virtual learning environment is that the course will be easier to set up and not require specialist web design skills. The virtual learning environment also has a number of inherent tools that can be utilised to make the course interactive. The availability and usability of these tools will vary depending on the VLE software being used, but generally will include online assessment tools, communication tools, such as bulletin boards or online chat rooms, the facility to submit online assignments and tracking functions. For more information, see the case study from Imperial College London, detailing the creation of an information literacy course in the VLE in Chapter 6.

Information literacy continues to be taught in many institutions through face-to-face classes alongside some form of web-based instruction. This style of teaching is known as blended learning. It can be highly effective, offering students valuable support via the Web to back up their face-to-face classes. However, it can easily be badly structured and integrated and lead to confusion and students having an unclear understanding of the role of both aspects of the teaching style.

Using the VLE for staff development

Another area of significant interest to librarians is using the VLE for staff development. Staff development in academic libraries is often well developed and includes programmes of training that often run throughout the year. As new electronic resources or systems become available, or procedures and processes evolve, so the need for staff development in most libraries is constant. Early on, a number of libraries realised the valuable role the VLE can play as a vehicle for staff development. Similar to its value for off-campus students, the VLE allows staff to access staff development resources at a time and place convenient to them. In many institutions, using the VLE for staff development also provides a useful way of ensuring library staff are familiar with the software that students are using.

Conclusion

This chapter has discussed how e-learning is changing the role of information professionals and offering them new opportunities to capitalise on their expertise. Through the delivery of information literacy programmes, which are both timely and integrated, partnerships with teaching and learning support staff can be strengthened. Librarians need to work with new groups of professionals, and they need to develop new skills, in particular teaching skills, which enable them to deliver these programmes, where appropriate using technology. E-learning is offering exciting and new possibilities which the library profession needs to reach out and seize. The key to success is to leave the library, build partnerships with teachers and learning technologists and infiltrate their networks. Chapter 1 showed how the library is no longer simply a physical building – it is a vast collection of digital resources, many accessible from the desktop, anywhere at any time. Librarians need to ensure their place in the virtual world of learning is as central as it was in the physical world.

Notes

1. See: *http://www.elit-conf.org/*

2. See: *http://www.leeds.ac.uk/bigblue/index.htm*

3. Backed by the UK government with £55m funding, the UK e-Universities (UKeU) were established to deliver online and worldwide the best degrees and degree-level learning that UK universities can provide. In March 2004 the HEFCE announced the UKeU was to be disbanded.

4. See: *http://www.mmu.ac.uk/services/library/bbconnect/*

5. To view the archives of this list: *http://www.jiscmail.ac.uk/lists/LIS-INFOLITERACY.html*

6. See: *http://www.netskills.ac.uk/*

7. See: *http://www.heacademy.ac.uk/*

8. More information available at: *http://www.alt.ac.uk/*

9. An up-to-date list of courses, workshops and conferences is available from: *http://www.ucisa.ac.uk/groups/tlig/courses.htm*

10. See: *http://www.ucisa.ac.uk/groups/tlig/teach/elearning04.htm*

References

Armstrong, C. J., Lonsdale, R. E., Stoker, D. A. and Urquhart, C. J. (2000) *JUSTEIS JISC usage surveys: trends in electronic information services*, Final Report – 1999/2000 Cycle. Available from: *http://www.dil.aber.ac.uk/dils/research/justeis/cyc1rep0.htm*.

Association of College and Research Libraries (ACRL) (2000) *Information Literacy Competency Standards for Higher Education.* Chicago: American Library Association. Available from: *http://www.ala.org/ala/acrl/acrlstandards/standards.pdf*.

Big Blue, The (2001) *The Big Blue: information skills for students*, Final Report, JISC/University of Leeds. Available from: *http://www.leeds.ac.uk/bigblue/finalreportful.html*.

Big Blue Connect (2003) *Final Report*. JISC: Manchester Metropolitan University. Available from: *http://www.library.mmu.ac.uk/bbconnect/finalreport.html*.

Borah, E., Kuchida, H., Lee, D., Lippincott, A. and Nagaraj, S. (2004) *Access paradox: an information literacy campaign response*, paper given at Elit 2004. Abstract available from: *http://www.elit-conf.org/elit2004/docs/sess3rmb3.html*.

Bruce, Christine (1997) *The Seven Faces of Information Literacy.* Adelaide: Auslib Press.

Council of Australian University Librarians (CAUL) (2001) *Information Literacy Standards*. Canberra: Council of Australian University Librarians. Available from: *http://www.caul.edu.au/caul-doc/Info LitStandards2001.doc*.

Gibbons, Susan (2003) 'Building upon the MyLibrary concept to better meet the information needs of college students', *D-Lib Magazine*, 9(3), March.

Martin, Allan (2003) 'Essential e-literacy. ICT in practice for Scottish Education', *Connected Online*, 9. Available from: *http://www .ltscotland.org.uk/connected/connected9/specialfeature/eliteracy.asp*.

Oliver, M., Sharpe, R., Duggleby, J., Jennings, D. and Kay, D. (2004) *Accrediting learning technologists: a review of the literature, schemes and programmes*. ALT Accreditation Project Report No. 1. Available from: *http://www.ucl.ac.uk/epd/alt-accreditation/Initial_review.doc*.

SCONUL (2003) *Information support for eLearning: principles and practices*, UKeU Briefing Paper. Available from: *http://www.sconul .ac.uk/pubs_stats/pubs/Information_Support_for_eLearning_Final.pdf*.

SCONUL (1999) *Information skills in higher education: a SCONUL position paper*. London: SCONUL. Available from: *http://www.sconul .ac.uk/pubs_stats/pubs/99104Rev1.doc*.

Secker, J. and Price, G. (2004) *Developing the e-literacy of academics: case studies from the London School of Economics and Political Science (LSE) and the Institute of Education*, paper delivered at Elit 2004 Conference. Abstract available from: *http://www.elit-conf.org/ elit2004/docs/sess2rmb1.html*.

Thomas, R. (2004) *E-literacy is more than information literacy*, paper delivered at Elit 2004. Abstract available from: *http://www.elit-conf.org/elit2004/docs/sess4rma1.html*.

Webber, S. and Johnston, B. (2000) 'Conceptions of information literacy: new perspectives and implications', *Journal of Information Science*, 26(6), 381–7.

Webber, S., Johnston, B. and Boon, S. (2004) *Information Literacy Weblog*, University of Sheffield. Available from: *http://ciquest.shef.ac .uk/infolit/*.

4

Copyright and licensing digital texts

Introduction

Knowledge of copyright, intellectual property rights and licensing issues is of crucial importance when linking virtual learning environments (VLEs) to digital library systems and resources. The responsibility for advising academic and other support staff about the most appropriate, and legal, use of electronic resources frequently falls to librarians. They also often have to answer general queries about copyright. Librarians are clearly not lawyers; however, as a librarian it is not uncommon to find that what you know about copyright is an awful lot more than many of your users will know!

This chapter is designed to be highly practical and answers many of the questions that you might have yourself or are likely to be asked by your users. First, there is an overview of copyright law in the UK, Australia and the US, examining the main characteristics of the law and highlighting major differences between the three countries. The chapter also includes a guide to copyright and the electronic environment, advice about using material from websites, linking to websites and also licensing text for inclusion within the VLE. The chapter is brought right up to date with information about new initiatives such as the 'Creative Commons' movement and new research being funded in the UK and Holland to explore copyright and the electronic environment (JISC/SURF, 2004). The chapter goes on to examine the copyright clearance and digitisation process that may need to be undertaken and issues surrounding outsourcing the production. Again it is brought up to date to include recent negotiations in the higher education sector in the UK, to include digitisation within the scope of the Copyright Licensing Agency (CLA) Higher Education Licence.

A brief guide to copyright

This book is not a definitive guide to copyright for librarians, for there are many good examples of these types of works already available. However, in the context of the virtual learning environment, this chapter briefly explains what copyright is and what type of resources it applies to. Copyright laws around the world do vary, so examples of further reading are given for the UK, Australia and the US. In the UK, works by Cornish (2001), Norman (2004) and Pedley (2000) are excellent guides written specifically for librarians and recent editions of such works have appeared as changes in the law necessitate. In the US, the American Library Association (ALA) have a large amount of copyright information on their website and have also published guides for librarians, such as those by Bruwelheid (1995), Johnston and Roark (1996) and Crews (2000). There are also several US books that specifically examine copyright in the digital environment, including Hoffman (2001) and Harris (2002). A recent publication by the Australian Copyright Council (2003) also examines the management of digital resources. For an overview of international copyright, Goldstein (2001) has produced a useful guide.

What is copyright?

Copyright is part of a wider group of rights known as 'intellectual property', which also includes designs, trademarks and patents. Its definition as a property right is significant because, as with other property, copyright can be bought, sold or transferred to another. Copyright gives the owner the exclusive right to activities such as copying the work and issuing copies of the work to the public, although the exact wording varies between countries. In many countries, licensing agreements allow individuals to go beyond the provisions set out in the law. Licences are, however, governed by contract law and are not part of copyright law.

For a work to be subject to copyright, Cornish (2001) argues it needs to meet the following three criteria:

- it must be original;
- it must be fixed in some way;
- it must be created by an author from a country which recognises copyright.

There is a wide spectrum of materials in which copyright exists, including some quite obvious sources like books, newspaper articles and the script of a play, but letters, web pages and even e-mail messages also fall into this description. Copyright also includes artistic works that can be not just paintings and sculpture, but also architectural plans, photographs and even a doodle drawn by a child in school.

Copyright does not exist in ideas. Therefore, copyright is not infringed if an individual takes another person's writings or drawings and adapts them, producing their own version of the work, provided it is original and the initial piece of work was not copied. Finally, copyright, unlike other intellectual property rights such as patents or trademarks, does not have to be registered in any way to apply. In the US, registration of copyright can be done through the US Copyright Office, but this is not compulsory. You will notice that many copyright works include the internationally recognised copyright symbol ©. However, this symbol merely acts as a reminder to the reader that copyright exists in the work, and because a work does not have this symbol never assume that it is not a copyright work.

Who owns copyright?

Copyright is generally owned by the primary author of a work; however, because it is a property right, it can be bought, sold or licensed to someone else. If there are joint authors to a work, then copyright can be owned jointly, but a contract would usually set out the primary author and owner of copyright. The only exception is work that is produced in the course of your employment, wherein the copyright lies with the employer. For example, under UK employment law, the work of a librarian employed to teach students information literacy at the University of London belongs not to the individual, but to the university.

International copyright agreements

Most countries throughout the world have copyright laws that protect the rights of their nationals. However, 'international copyright law' does not exist to automatically protect an author's writings throughout the entire world and protection in a particular country depends on the national laws of that country. Most countries in the world do offer protection to foreign works under certain conditions. Over the years, these conditions have been greatly simplified by international copyright treaties and conventions. The first international recognition of copyright was the Berne Convention for the Protection of Literary and Artistic Works issued in 1886. Before this, works by foreign nationals were not protected outside of their country of origin, so a work published in France, for example, could be freely reproduced in the UK. The US did not sign up to the Convention because it would have required major changes to its copyright laws. However, in 1952 in Geneva, UNESCO developed the Universal Copyright Convention (UCC) to cater for those countries, such as the US, that did not adhere to Berne.

Since 1967, the convention has been administered by WIPO (the World Intellectual Property Organisation). WIPO is a specialised agency of the United Nations defining itself as:

> An international organization dedicated to promoting the use and protection of works of the human spirit. These works – intellectual property – are expanding the bounds of science and technology and enriching the world of the arts.[1]

The legislation

The major copyright and associated laws in the US, the UK and Australia are briefly examined in this section.

In the US the 1976 Copyright Act remains in force and gives the owner of copyright the exclusive right to do and to authorise others to do the following:

- to reproduce the work in copies or phonorecords;
- to prepare derivative works based upon the work;
- to distribute copies or phonorecords of the work to the public by sale or other transfer of ownership, or by rental, lease, or lending;
- to perform the work publicly, in the case of literary, musical, dramatic, and choreographic works, pantomimes, and motion pictures and other audiovisual works;
- to display the copyrighted work publicly, in the case of literary, musical, dramatic, and choreographic works, pantomimes, and pictorial, graphic, or sculptural works, including the individual images of a motion picture or other audiovisual work;
- and for sound recordings, to perform the work publicly by a digital audio transmission.

However, librarians in the US need to be aware of a number of other laws relating to copyright. For example, in 1998, the US signed into law the Digital Millennium Copyright Act (DMCA). The legislation was designed to implement two 1996 World Intellectual Property Organisation (WIPO) treaties: the WIPO Copyright Treaty and the WIPO Performances and Phonograms Treaty. It also addressed a number of other significant copyright-related issues. Section 1201 is of most relevance to librarians for it prohibits the 'circumvention' of any effective 'technological protection measure' (e.g a password or form of encryption) used by a copyright holder to restrict access to its material.

Another Act of relevance to US librarians, particularly those involved with the provision of distance learning materials, is the Technology, Education and Copyright Harmonisation Act (the TEACH Act) 2002. This Act allows copyright protected materials to be used in distance education, including on websites and by other digital means, without permission from the copyright owner and without payment of royalties. However, the law does expect educational institutions to undertake numerous procedures to comply with the Act. The ALA have produced an excellent overview of the meaning and importance of this Act on their website.[2]

In the UK, the legislation in force is the Copyright, Designs and Patents Act of 1988. The full text of the Act is available on the Web.[3] However, since 1988, Statutory Instruments (SI) have been used to make many amendments to the original Act. To ensure you are looking at the full and up-to-date version of the law, you must also consult the SIs. The 1988 Act defines copyright as:

> … a property right which subsists … in the following descriptions of work –
> (a) original literary, dramatic, musical or artistic works,
> (b) sound recordings, films, broadcasts or cable programmes, and
> (c) the typographical arrangement of published editions.

Australian copyright law is governed by the 1968 Copyright Act, although the legislation has been amended many times since this date. In 2000, two significant amendments to the law were enacted including the recognition of moral rights – the Copyright Amendment (Moral Rights) Act and the Copyright Amendment (Digital Agenda) Act. The full text is available on the Web with all the amendments included.[4] The significance of these changes is discussed later in the chapter.

Duration of copyright protection

Copyright is not protected indefinitely in most countries of the world and will expire after a set period of time. Duration of copyright is an area where the law differs between countries, for example between the UK, US and Australia (see Table 4.1). In the UK (and the US) copyright protection for literary, dramatic, musical or artistic work is provided:

- to the author of the work, the person who created it during their lifetime;
- to their executors for 70 years after the author's death;
- for the typographical arrangement of a published edition for 25 years from the date of publication.

In the US, the duration of copyright was extended from 50 to 70 years in 1978; however, this did not offer the same length of protection for works published before this date. This led to the Sonny Bono Copyright Term Extension Act of 1998, which extended the copyright of works first published before 1978. Meanwhile in Australia, copyright in literary works is protected for the life of an author and then for 50 years after their death.

The duration of copyright law can vary depending on the format of the material. For example, UK law offers protection for films for 70 years after the last to die of:

- the principal director;
- the author of the screenplay;
- the author of the dialogue;
- the composer of the music created for and used in the film.

Also in the UK, sound recordings, broadcasts, cable programmes and computer-generated works have copyright protection for 50 years after the end of the year in which they were first made, released or first broadcast or included in a cable programme service. If copyright has expired works can be freely copied, but it is wise to check the law in your country and to check for variations between the different formats.

The permitted acts and fair dealing

Copyright laws throughout the world are not all-pervasive and make provision for some level of copying under specific terms and conditions. UK law and the laws of many Commonwealth countries, such as

Table 4.1	Duration of copyright for UK

Work	Duration
Literary and artistic works	70 years after death of author
Films	70 years[*]
Sounds, recordings and broadcasts	50 years after broadcast
Typographical arrangement	25 years
Anonymous works	70 years after first publication

*After last to die of director, author of screenplay, author of dialogue and composer of music – see p. 80 for details.

Australia and Canada, have a concept known as 'fair dealing' which sets out a number of permitted acts that are defences in a court of law, not rights. In the US law there is a similar concept known as Fair Use, which is generally far more flexible.

In the UK the law states that in order to infringe copyright, you must copy a 'substantial' part of a work, therefore copying an insubstantial part would not arguably infringe copyright. However, as with many terms in UK copyright law, the term 'substantial' is not defined to mean a particular amount taken from a work and will vary depending on the nature of the work. Publishers generally agree that copying 10 per cent or less might constitute insubstantial, but there are no agreed limits. Additionally it would depend on what is being copied. So a number of pages copied from the middle of a thriller, for example, may be insubstantial in terms of size and content. However, reproducing the final three pages of the same thriller where the culprit is revealed could easily be considered substantial.

This area of the law was changed in October 2003, following the UK's enactment of the European Union's Copyright Directive (2001/09/EC).[5] The law was changed in several ways but, most significantly for libraries, copying for private research and study had to be for non-commercial purposes. In the UK, 'fair dealing' permits copying for three purposes, including for:

- 'research and private study' (must be non-commercial research);
- criticism and review;
- reporting of current events;
- public administration purposes.

An individual conducting private non-commercial research or study is allowed to copy an insubstantial part of the work for these purposes.

Individuals, often using self-service photocopiers in libraries, frequently undertake this type of copying. So, for example, non-commercial purposes might include: a student who photocopies a journal article to read as part of their degree, or the private researcher undertaking family history who photocopies a newspaper article relating to one of their ancestors. Increasingly, individuals want to make digital copies of these articles, and this can also be undertaken for private research and study. So, for example, the lecturer who scans an article onto his desktop PC for his own private research can do this under the fair dealing provision. For copying beyond these limits, universities, schools and businesses in the UK obtain licences from the UK Copyright Licensing Agency (CLA) for their staff or students. Under these licences, multiple copies of portions of copyrighted works can be made for educational purposes. This is discussed in more detail later in this chapter.

In Australia the grounds for fair dealing are fairly similar and are specified as:

- research and study;
- review and criticism;
- 'reporting the news';
- legal advice (although the crown is deemed to own copyright in federal statutes, and each state in state statutes).

Australian law is more specific than the UK, guaranteeing that fair dealing applies if you photocopy either 'not more than one chapter', or 'less than 10%' of a book or journal.

Fair Use

In US law the concept known as 'Fair Use' is much more liberal about what can be copied. Fair use allows, in a limited manner, the use of copyright protected materials for purposes of parody, news reports, comedic acts, research and education. The law considers four factors in determining if fair use is applicable as a defence, including:

- the purpose and character of the use, including whether use is of a commercial nature or is for not-for-profit educational purposes;
- the nature of the copyrighted work;
- the amount and substantiality of the portion used in relation to the copyrighted work as a whole;

- the effect of the use upon the potential market for or value of the copyrighted work.

There has been considerable discussion among US librarians about the fair use concept in both the print and electronic environments. The CONFU (Conference on Fair Use) was formed in 1994 and it is hosted by the US Patent and Trademark Office. CONFU has led to informal discussions of the parameters of fair use in the digital environment in educational, scholarly and library settings. Its membership included copyright proprietors, producers and users. CONFU issued guidelines which some libraries adopted. The ALA published a statement in November 2003 regarding fair use and electronic reserves (or electronic short loan as this is known in the UK).[6] This is discussed in more detail later in the chapter. There are also numerous Internet resources available, such as those produced by Stanford University Library which has a website devoted to copyright and fair use.[7] These are all valuable resources for US librarians.

Copyright, digital rights and the electronic environment

For a short while in the 1990s there was an idea circulating that copyright did not exist on the Internet and that with the enormous explosion in types and amounts of information being made freely available copyright would become a thing of the past. That idea has quickly dissipated and digital rights have in fact become a hot topic. Digital rights management (DRM) is currently an issue many organisations are grappling with. In the UK, JISC has recently commissioned a study to investigate the DRM issues affecting the higher and further education communities.[8] Similarly in the Netherlands, the SURF Foundation has also recently commissioned research in this field.[9] In recognition that copyright and the Internet is increasingly an international issue, JISC and SURF have combined forces to launch a joint project in June 2004, entitled *Copyright Doesn't Stop at the Border* (JISC/SURF, June 2004). With funding for a five-part programme of research which is likely to clarify many of the copyright issues discussed in this chapter, the programme will specifically:

- create a toolkit to help draw up copyright agreements between authors and publishers;

- provide support to universities in formulating (or reformulating) copyright policy, providing examples, good practices and practical guidelines;

- develop a user-friendly, international knowledge bank intended to contain information about publishers' copyright policies;

- provide communication on the subject of copyright, including a 'know your rights' campaign to increase awareness among universities and authors about their rights;

- analyse copyright aspects in the Netherlands and UK with regard to 'open access', i.e. the free availability of scientific information over the Internet.

Meanwhile, DRM software solutions could become increasingly common in the future, as companies seek to protect their intellectual property. It is now commonplace to see websites using techniques such as watermarking of images to prevent them being downloaded and re-used by individuals. Material that may have once been made available freely on the Internet is now often kept locked behind encryption techniques which only allow authorised users to download it. However, to counteract this movement, the Creative Commons movement, where material can be licensed for public use, is also fast gaining ground.

As librarians, we all realise that copyright applies equally in the electronic environment and it is a mistake to believe that copyright does not exist on the Internet. However, many individuals still believe that they can download material and reuse it without proper acknowledgement. When building course websites, some academics or course designers might be tempted to download material from the Internet and use it within their site. As a literary work, you should advise them to treat all websites as copyright works and only copy without permission under the terms of fair dealing, or fair use, depending on your country of origin.

More and more often, websites have clear copyright statements, conditions or terms of use or explicit licences associated with them. These clearly set out what you can and cannot do with material on the Web. Often, simply by accessing material on a particular website you are agreeing to abide by their terms and conditions. Two examples of websites with explicit copyright statements are given below.

The UK National Archives

The first example is the National Archives (formerly the Public Record Office): *http://www.www.nationalarchives.gov.uk/*. The copyright statement on this website is clear (see Figure 4.1) in that it states that the contents of the site are protected by Crown Copyright. The site is clear that images are to be treated separately and anyone wanting to reuse images should contact the Image Library and will be subject to a fee. Images are discussed in more detail later in this chapter, but it is increasingly common to find that specific resources such as images are protected in this way because of their potential commercial benefit.

Figure 4.1 The National Archives copyright notice

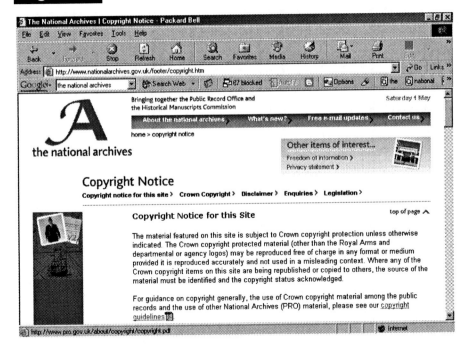

The Amazon UK website

The second example is the Amazon UK website (*http://www.amazon .co.uk*) which will be familiar to many people (see Figure 4.2).

Figure 4.2 Amazon conditions of use and sale

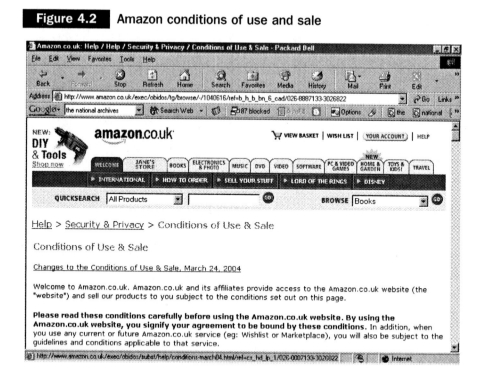

This website has what are termed 'Conditions of Use and Sale' which may be less familiar. However, you are asked to read these conditions very carefully before using the website and Amazon will assume that you have read and understood them. They grant users what they call a 'limited licence' which permits:

> personal use of this website, but not to download (other than page caching) or modify it, or any portion of it, except with express written consent of Amazon.co.uk.[10]

Amazon also are clear that:

> All content included on the website, such as text, graphics, logos, button icons, images, audio clips, digital downloads, data compilations, and software, is the property of Amazon.co.uk, its affiliates or its content suppliers and is protected by United Kingdom and international copyright and database right laws.

Ideally, it is recommended before accessing, but specifically before using, downloading or copying any information from a website, the terms of use, copyright statement or licence should be examined.

Linking to websites

Hyperlinks are the basis of the World Wide Web and far more preferable from a copyright perspective, as you refer individuals to material rather than copy it. However, linking is not without problems and there are some general rules you should follow to avoid copyright issues. Wherever possible, linking should be 'surface links' – to the home page of a website, rather than 'deep links' to the body of a website. In fact both the two examples used previously, the National Archives and Amazon, explicitly state in their copyright notice that they encourage hyperlinking to the home page of their website. Commercial websites such as Amazon will often require that links are established to their home page because this is the designated 'front door' into the site and guarantees that advertisements and new information are seen by the user. Additionally, links to the home page are easier to maintain and less likely to become 'dead' links.

One of the potential problems with hyperlinking is not infringing copyright, but that it can be construed as 'passing off'. Passing off is a common law tort whereby someone attempts to pass off another person's products or services as their own. So, for example, if a deep link to an article is added from one website to another, bypassing the home page, it may appear as if the article originated from the referring website. A frequently cited UK case from the late 1990s involved two rival newspapers, *The Shetland Times* and *The Shetland News*, where objections were made to the use of hyperlinking. The defendant, *The Shetland News*, used headlines from a rival newspaper on its own website. Thinking they were viewing articles posted by *The Shetland News*, users could view an entire *Shetland Times* article by clicking on a link. In fact, they had followed a deep link to within the *Times* site, bypassing customer service information and advertising. The case was eventually settled out of court in 1997 when the links were removed.

One technique to avoid 'passing off' a website as your own content is to ensure that links open within a new web browser window. This is particularly important within a virtual learning environment where links may open within the same window by default. Some websites will have an explicit statement that forbids the use of certain types of links, such as deep or frame links. Frame links are where a link to a website opens within the frame and might be confused as being part of the site where the link originated. Frame links can be set up fairly easily within some VLE software, for example many versions of WebCT use frames. Links to external websites by default will open in the WebCT frame and may appear as if they are an integral part of the course website. In this case, hyperlinks should be set up to open in a new window, which can be easily done.

In some instances, particularly where transient information appears on websites or if there is a concern that the material might be removed at a later stage, teaching staff may insist that they download material rather than link to it. This will usually require obtaining copyright permission and sometimes this responsibility will fall to a librarian. In other cases, staff may ask for advice about seeking permission. Further advice is available later in this chapter. Nevertheless, do not assume that if permission is required this will always be difficult to obtain and cost a large amount of money. Many educational websites will freely grant permission for other academics to use their material. In the first instance, check any licences or copyright statements on a website to determine the conditions of use. If you need to request permission, contact details are usually included on the bottom of web pages. Appendix 1 contains a sample letter which could be sent to the owner of a website to request permission to download material for educational use.

Using images from the Web

One of the easiest things to download are images from other websites. Search engines such as Google allow users to search specifically for images, making them easy to identify. Even those with limited technical knowledge can download images from the Web and reuse them in their own website. However, you should be aware that this constitutes copying and is infringing copyright law. If you wish to use a particular image from another website, permission should always be obtained from the copyright holder. Increasingly, as previously noted, commercial website owners are including a watermark or some other digital rights management system in images to discourage illegal copying, but also to allow owners to track down illegal copying.

A true story: a senior academic wished to reuse an image he found in an article written by a colleague, and because it was for publication in a journal and he knew the individual concerned, he approached him to ask for copyright permission. The response he received was somewhat surprising, but then again perhaps not! The academic replied that he would happily grant him permission to reuse the image – except that he himself had downloaded it from the Web and couldn't remember where he had obtained it. Consequently, the academic decided to find an alternative image rather than risk publishing the image and having its original owner see it and object.

So what is the solution? Generally, it is recommended that when constructing your website, for educational use, or for any other purpose, you should try to ensure you own the rights to all the resources you wish to use. So, where possible, if you want to use images to illustrate your site, use your own images. Photographs that you own can easily be scanned, or perhaps the simplest answer is to obtain a digital camera and then take your own photographs. If you don't have the time or resources to do this there are also numerous websites available that provide free images that can be reused for non-commercial purposes. One such example is freeimages.co.uk (*http://www.freeimages.co.uk*). Such websites as this do have terms and conditions attached to their use. The website cited asks that:

> A link (or textural credit in non-web applications) to our commercial site is required where an image is used.[11]

It is also recommended that if you want to use images in your website, you should investigate the digital image collections available in your institution. Collections of images on all sorts of topics are increasingly being licensed for educational use. For example, your institution may subscribe to a commercial image collection such as the Education Image Gallery (*http://edina.ac.uk/eig/*) available through the Edina service hosted at Edinburgh University. The gallery is specifically designed for further and higher education use and includes thousands of images from the Getty collection. The images are copyright-cleared for teaching, learning and research and can be used in web-based or printed materials. Many institutions also have their own digitised image collections, which can be used without copyright permission. Finally, if you really must use someone else's image, then ask them for permission first!

Creative Commons

When discussing copyright and the Internet the 'Creative Commons' movement (*http://creativecommons.org/*) is gaining considerable support in the education sector. The movement argues that it is trying to strike a balance between an overly restricted world where no information can ever be copied, and one in which anarchy prevails and those who create content are left vulnerable to exploitation. The movement was founded in 2001 by the Center for Public Domain (*http://www.centerpd.org/*) in the US. Put simply:

> Creative Commons has developed a Web application that helps people dedicate their creative works to the public domain – or retain their copyright while licensing them as free for certain uses, on certain conditions.[12]

The licences can be used with various forms of creative works, such as websites, scholarship, music, film, photography, literature, courseware, etc. The licences are being developed in machine-readable form, so that people can use the Creative Commons search application to find material that can be reused without additional costs. The initiative was launched in the UK in January 2004, although there is still some uncertainty about the validity of Creative Commons licences outside the US. These forms of licences are being considered as part of the JISC DRM study, mentioned earlier in this chapter. The final report from this project, due in late 2004, should include further information about this topic.[13]

Linking to or downloading from electronic library resources

Your university or institution library will subscribe to a range of digital resources that are licensed for use by your staff and students. These can be anything from image collections, such as the Education Image Gallery discussed above, to electronic journal collections such as JSTOR or specialist subject indexes such as EconLit or Sociological Abstracts. Establishing links to these resources from within the VLE is an excellent way of directing students to use library resources to exploit these collections, and usually does not necessitate paying additional copyright fees. Subject specialists in the library are well placed to advise academic staff about the inclusion of links to such resources within their course website. These can be tailored according to the individual course, and there may be links to 'top level' resources. For example, a link can be added to access the EconLit database alongside some advice about how to search this resource. Alternatively the link could be a deep link to a specific resource, such as a journal article that students are required to read.

Digital library resources are subject to licence agreements that should be consulted for information about deep linking and whether they allow material to be downloaded and reused within the VLE. Most electronic journal providers allow 'article level' linking from course websites, and provide instructions on how these are established. This type of integration between the VLE and electronic resources is extremely valuable to students and to staff. It is also an area where librarians may need to provide support and training for staff. Chapter 6 therefore includes detailed information about how to establish article level links from many of the major electronic journal providers. Generally, establishing links to these resources is unproblematic; however, if teaching staff wish to download material such as journal articles and upload it directly into their course website, this should be undertaken with care – and after a detailed scrutiny of the licence agreement to check that this is permitted.

Multimedia resources

Increasingly, teaching staff wish to use audio and video resources within the VLE. In the past, such items may have been deposited in the library collection and made available to students to borrow or use within the library. However, digital technology facilitates the distribution of this material far more easily. A variety of video and audio formats exist, which allow material to be downloaded or accessed via the Internet. An increasing amount of audio and video collections is available on the Internet and staff may wish to use these resources in their teaching. In these cases, follow the instructions for using websites and where possible advise them to link to this material rather than downloading it. Digital sound or video collections may exist within your institution that can be used in teaching. For example, the London School of Economics and Political Science occasionally record and digitise public lectures held at the School, which staff are able to incorporate into their course website. Digital video collections may also be licensed for use at your institution. For example, Education Media Online (*http://www.emol.ac.uk/*), another service from Edina, is funded by JISC and is a set of film and video collections which subscribing institutions can use freely for teaching, learning and research.

Generally, 'born digital' audio and video collections are less problematic and difficulties usually occur when staff wish to use existing multimedia resources, such as excerpts from films, television broadcasts or sound recordings. Any pre-recorded videos, DVDs or sound recordings purchased by individuals have associated licensing agreements which forbid them being shown outside the home. In the UK, copyright permission is required for even short extracts. Some small production companies will grant permission for their material to be used for free, but others will charge a fee, which can be based on the length of the extract.

In the UK, television and radio broadcasts can be recorded for educational use by institutions that hold a specific licence called the Educational Recording Agency (ERA) Licence. The licence allows TV and radio excerpts to be copied into digital format. An excerpt may be shown but not edited to incorporate other material. Any excerpt must be clearly identified with the programme title, date of recording and channel, together with a statement saying it was recorded under the terms of the ERA Licence. Some UK higher education institutions are now distributing this material from the VLE, which is interpreted to mean 'classroom use'. To comply with the licence, the material is not distributed beyond the university campus.

Using teaching materials in the VLE

Lecturers frequently wish to make their own teaching resources available to students in the virtual learning environment. Students appreciate being able to download lecture notes or PowerPoint slides when they have missed a lecture or for revision purposes. Teaching staff find that the VLE provides a convenient place to deposit these resources and means that students are less likely to come knocking on their doors when they miss a lecture. Some teaching staff are concerned that making these resources available may discourage students from attending lectures, but generally this does not seem to be a widespread problem. Just think for yourself if you ever miss a seminar and a colleague brings you the handout – very few PowerPoint slides truly make sense unless you have attended the event, and it has been said that the lecturer who can be replaced by PointPoint slides probably deserves to be replaced! Seriously though, to counteract this problem, lecturers often only make these resources available after the event has taken place, and generally only make a lecture outline, rather than full notes, available.

From a copyright perspective you might think that there are very few issues associated with making teaching resources available from the VLE. However, do bear in mind that staff do sometimes use resources such as images or even video within PowerPoint presentations that they don't own the rights to and may have found on the Internet. Material that is shown within a lecture is more difficult to oversee, but once it has been uploaded into the VLE it is more visible. It is advisable for library staff in conjunction with other copyright experts in the institution to produce copyright guidelines to ensure PowerPoint and other teaching materials are not infringing. Examples of universities who have produced such guidelines are Curtin University of Technology[14] in Australia, Penn State University[15] in the US and the London School of Economics and Political Science[16] in the UK.

Under UK law, special provision is made for copying for examination purposes. For the purposes of setting, communicating or answering the questions in closed exams anything may be done with copyright materials (except for music) without permission. Many institutions are increasingly using assessment tools available in the VLE, such as quizzes or surveys that are available in WebCT, or specific online assessment tools such as QuestionMark Perception. For these purposes, copyrighted material can often be included.

The need for copyright clearance

In general you should assume that you will need permission to download and reuse an item within the VLE, unless:

- the items are out of copyright;
- the individual who wishes to use the material is the copyright holder; or
- your organisation is the copyright holder.

You should be wary of academic staff publications where they are the author of the material, for example book chapters or journal articles, but not necessarily the copyright owner. Often they will have assigned certain rights to their publisher, so it is important to check their publishing contract or the terms of agreement. If they wish to use material that a colleague has produced, where copyright will lie with your university or organisation, they should be advised that it is courteous to discuss this with the colleague before using the material. Remember, they will also require permission to adapt material produced by someone else.

Copyright and electronic reserves

Chapter 1 contains considerable discussion about the development of electronic reserves collections or, as they are more commonly called in the UK, electronic course packs. In both the UK and Australia, copying or scanning copyright works for classroom use goes beyond what is permitted by law and is consequently governed by a licence. In the US, the situation is more permissive and many libraries claim that scanning for electronic reserves falls into the remit of Fair Use.

In the UK, the Copyright Licensing Agency (CLA) administers licences for multiple copying and they offer both paper-to-paper and digitisation licences for schools, further and higher education and also for business use. This section draws on the author's experience obtaining copyright clearance and digitising readings in-house within an institution and using the HERON Service. In particular, it draws on experiences at the London School of Economics and research which was conducted at University College, London (UCL) to investigate the issues associated with providing access to core readings in electronic format.[17] The project led to the establishment of a pilot service at UCL and the author subsequently has expanded and developed a similar service at the LSE.

Digital copyright in the UK

The CLA is the UK's reprographic rights agency, representing a large number of UK publishers and other rightsholders. Librarians are often familiar with this organisation because it issues paper-to-paper licences that if purchased by an organisation permit multiple copying to be undertaken beyond the scope of fair dealing.

In 1999 the CLA issued their first digitisation licence for higher education. The licence came about following several JISC projects investigating on-demand publishing or electronic reserves, which were discussed in more detail in Chapter 1. The CLA licence made provision for scanning of work so that it could be distributed via a secure network to authorised persons at an institution. The licence is free to take out; however, it is currently based on a transactional basis, and all material scanned under the licence needs to be copyright cleared. In the early days of the licence it was agreed that the price was to be based on the length of the article (number of pages) and the number of students to which it would be distributed. JISC and the Publishers Association made recommendations that no more than 5 pence per page per student should be charged for digital permissions. However, the number of publishers charging 5 pence per page or less has declined rapidly, and it is not uncommon for publishers to charge far more than this amount.

Currently the CLA is reviewing the Higher Education Digitisation Licence, in particular the transactional nature of this licence. In January 2004 the CLA held a consultation meeting with the community, where the higher education sector strongly recommended that a blanket licence approach be adopted. The CLA has also recently issued a trial blanket licence for further education, covering both scanning and photocopying. At the time of writing this book, the CLA has entered into negotiations with two bodies representing the higher education sector, Universities UK (UUK) and the Standing Conference of Principals (SCOP). There are indications that a joint scanning and photocopying licence will be issued on a trial basis in late 2004/early 2005. Under the current model, expansion of electronic reserves services in the UK is not cost effective. Moreover, the CLA recognises that a transactional licence is not ideal. In 2001, UUK, which represents the higher education sector in the UK, brought a case against the CLA before the Copyright Tribunal. The case was successful and the Tribunal maintained that the transactional nature of the higher education photocopying licence was restrictive. This led to the inclusion of course pack copying into the blanket licence.

Australia also provides a useful example of where a blanket licence approach to digitisation is working. In 2001, following an amendment to the copyright law, core readings could be scanned for educational use. The work is undertaken under a licence issued from Australia's reprographic rights organisation, the Copyright Agency Limited (CAL). It is anticipated that such a licence might soon be offered in the UK, which will undoubtedly lead to an enormous growth in the demand for electronic reserves.

Advice on obtaining copyright clearance

Even if a blanket licence were to exist in the UK, publishers are not obliged to be part of it. In both Australia and the US there are still times when it is necessary to obtain copyright clearance to use materials. Therefore, this section discusses the set-up and structure of a copyright clearance service within libraries and the type of work that is often undertaken.

A number of UK libraries have already established centres or units for copyright clearance work. This is often associated with paper course pack provision or short loan off-print collections. For example, at University College, London[18] the Subject Support Unit was established by Library Services in the mid-1990s to undertake copyright clearance for the newly established paper course pack service. The unit has now been restructured and renamed as the Teaching and Learning Support Section, taking responsibility for both print and digital copyright clearance requests. Similarly, the Electronic Copyright and Digitisation Unit (ECDU) was established at the University of Derby in the 1990s to obtain copyright clearance for core readings.[19] However, staffing in many libraries is such that resources are not available to undertake copyright clearance work. In the UK this work can be outsourced to the HERON Service (discussed in Chapter 1), which will obtain copyright clearance and digitise core readings for use in further and higher education.

If resources and staff are available to undertake copyright permissions in-house there are many issues that need to be considered. The time taken to obtain copyright permission can vary, depending on individual copyright holders. The first port of call for a permission request will often be your national reprographic rights organisation. The CLA hold a mandate for the majority of UK publishers and permissions obtained via the CLA can take a matter of days. The CLA website contains details, updated regularly, of excluded works and publishers that are not covered by their licences.[20] They also include a list of US publishers that are covered by their licence. Permission requests can be submitted via e-mail, using the CLARCS (Copyright Licensing Agency Rapid Clearance Service). For many US works it is also possible to obtain copyright clearance from the Copyright Clearance Center (CCC) in the US.[21] Institutions can set up an account with the CCC and where publishers have mandated them, permission for electronic and paper copies can be granted online immediately. In Australia, the Copyright Agency Limited (CAL) offers a Copyright Express service via their website and can approve copying by individuals who do not hold one of their licences or copying that goes beyond the limits of their licences.[22] Once again, permissions can be approved online.

There may be instances where lecturers require readings from publishers not covered by your reprographic rights organisation. Alternatively you may wish to contact a publisher directly when dealing with an 'author permission'. Author permissions are where the author of a work wishes to obtain permission to use the material. In these cases you will need to approach the publishers directly and responses can take anything from several weeks to several months, and sometimes a response may not be received. In the first instance, a publisher's website is usually a good source of information for details about their rights and permissions department. Follow the instructions provided here to submit your request. This may mean faxing the publisher or completing an online form. Small publishers may not have a specific department dealing with rights, in which case you will need to use a general contact e-mail to identify the correct person. Any permissions received either by e-mail or letter should be kept on file for the duration of the licence period.

There are a number of issues to consider when considering establishing an electronic course pack/digital text service:

- staff availability and expertise – both professional and clerical support are vital if this service is going to be run in-house. Also consider that outsourcing to HERON still requires a considerable degree of administrative support;
- equipment availability;
- budget for paying copyright costs – will the costs be charged to academic departments? Can the costs be top-sliced from departmental budgets? Will a central budget be provided?
- server space for readings;
- administration – such services invariably involve copious paperwork and a robust database or administrative process that helps you track permissions requests and manage the licences is essential.

When deciding whether to obtain copyright clearance you should note:

- You should not scan readings for classroom use without permission from the copyright holders.
- Publishers are not obliged to grant digital rights and some have an outright policy not to allow material from their textbooks to be digitised.
- Obtaining permission for electronic environments can take longer than obtaining paper clearances as some publishers still feel cautious about the electronic environment.
- In some instances, copyright lies with authors rather than publishers and individuals can be notoriously difficult to trace.

Licence models for digital texts

A number of different licence models exist for digital texts and some publishers have created their own models which may take into account actual usage of the material. In the UK, following detailed studies by JISC and the Publishers Association back in the late 1990s as part of the eLib Programme, two types of licence for digital readings were devised which are quite different to the way other electronic resources are licensed. The two models are known as:

- textbook purchase substitution/bookshop model;
- library purchase substitution.

The textbook substitution model is based on the notion of digital readings being an electronic course pack, analogous with a paper course pack that is a prepared set of readings for students on a particular course. This model is sometimes called the 'bookshop model'. The premise is that students are using the digital text in place of a textbook which they would otherwise have gone out and purchased. Therefore, publishers are seeking to maintain their profits and ensure that the pricing of the licence covers any potential reduction in the sale of textbooks. The general model is that readings are paid for on the basis of the length of the article and the number of students on the course. This is the most common type of licence currently being offered to academic institutions either through the CLA, CCC or directly from publishers.

The advantages of this licence are:

- that you only pay for the number of students on the course so it is possible to license readings for small numbers of students and so specialist courses are not penalised;
- that it allows flexibility when teaching staff update reading lists and payments for materials are only made for a limited period of time.

However, there are a number of disadvantages, including:

- it can be difficult to predict the exact numbers of students on a course, in particular for new courses;
- there are no economies of scale, so that when licensing readings for large courses, high costs can be entailed;
- when readings are required for several academic years they need to be renewed each year, with a new licence fee being paid.

The second type of licence is analogous with the purchase of a book by a library and is generally used for readings which a student would not have been expected to purchase, but might have been purchased by the library as background reading. This model allows the reading to be recommended to any student at an institution and is generally a more cost-effective way of licensing electronic texts. Readings licensed under this model are often obtained for five years, which again can make them more cost-effective. Only a limited number of publishers offer this type of licence, an example being Oxford University Press.

Despite a JISC/Publishers Association recommendation back in 1997 to fix prices to no more than 5p per page per students, pricing policies are set by individual publishers and there is enormous variation (Bide et al., 1997). The standard model of pricing is to base the cost on the length of the articles in terms of numbers of pages and the number of students on the course for which the reading has been recommended. This model has a number of inherent problems, specifically because providing access to core readings in digital format is primarily motivated by the desire to ensure large numbers of students can obtain access to a key text. However, under the current pricing model, the price increases in line with the increase in numbers of students on the course. Therefore there are no cost benefits to making a reading available to a large group of students as opposed to a smaller group.

Electronic books (e-books), particularly electronic versions of textbooks, are one development that may alter this market. There is an increasing number of e-book deals that are available to subscribing libraries. These are discussed in Chapter 1, but rather than paying for individual titles, publishers are making larger collections available under licence. In general the collection is licensed on an institution-wide basis, and the pricing model is more similar to that of electronic journals.

Permission requests: what to include

Appendix 2 presents a sample letter that can be used when seeking to obtain copyright permission to use a digitised version of a textbook. Generally, when trying to obtain permission it is sensible to include information about:

- where the material will be hosted – it might be useful to include the URL of the site;
- access to the site – password protection facilities, how you ensure only authorised persons will access the material;
- the format of the material you wish to make available: PDF, Word documents, XML, etc.;
- duration of copyright you are requesting – whether the material will be made available for a limited period of time;
- who will be accessing the material – if it's for a specific course, how many students are on the course, who is teaching it, what is the name of the course?

Digitisation

Many publishers are happy for you to digitise the material yourself, provided it is an exact representation of the original published work and not modified in any way. Other publishers may request that you use their own digital copy of the work or obtain a copy from a trusted repository, digitised to a particular quality standard.

In-house digitisation

In-house digitisation on the surface may appear to be an obvious solution, but you should consider carefully the staffing and equipment costs of such a service. These will vary depending on the quality of the files you are aiming to produce and the volume of material that you are hoping to purchase, but the minimum requirements for in-house digitisation would be:

- dedicated PC and scanner;
- robust scanner, preferably with sheet feeder;
- dedicated server space (with files typically 1 MB in size, ensure the server has sufficient capacity for expansion);
- staff time to undertake scanning.

The purchase of the equipment may actually be the least of the problems associated with in-house digitisation. One of the greatest challenges may be finding staff time to scan the material. The equipment also needs to be set up to ensure that material is scanned to an appropriate resolution that allows it to be read on screen or printed out, but does not result in excessively large files. Another important decision is whether to use optical character recognition (OCR) software to convert the material to text format. This will drastically reduce the file size, but does take additional time as documents need to be proofread to ensure errors have not been introduced and to remove artefacts such as line-break hyphens and page numbers.

Outsourced digitisation

Increasingly in the UK, institutions are looking to outsource digitisation of core readings. This is particularly useful if staff and equipment are not available. In the UK the primary service offering digitisation of such readings is the HERON Service, which is now part of Ingenta UK. Outsourcing has several advantages, in particular:

- staff time and equipment is not required to carry out the digitisation work;
- less staff training in new skills is necessary;
- the material does not have to be physically held by the library – such services generally acquire clean photocopies from the British Library;
- better quality files are usually received – including text files which are extremely time consuming to produce in-house.

There are several disadvantages to using such a service, including:

- material can take longer to process than in-house;
- the service is often less flexible than an in-house service;
- there may be higher overall costs: for example, the HERON Service typically charge approximately £30 per item for digitisation, in addition to any copyright costs;
- if your collection has specialist material that cannot be obtained from the British Library it may be necessary to supply a digital copy or photocopy of the article – so some staff time is still associated with outsourced production.

There are obvious advantages to national or international trust repositories that can supply institutions with high-quality digitised materials. In the UK, the HERON Service is trying to build its reputation in this role. However, outside the UK, generally universities are continuing to scan articles individually as they are needed. The files have the advantage that once they have been scanned they can be reused. However, with an increasing number of electronic journals and e-books, it is anticipated that demand for electronic reserves services may eventually reduce dramatically.

Conclusion

This chapter has examined a wide range of copyright and licensing issues associated with the use of library resources in a virtual learning environment. As librarians you may be asked to advise academic staff on a range of issues and ensure that where they are using resources they are not infringing copyright. This chapter cannot hope to answer all the questions you will encounter, but it should provide a good grounding in many of the major topics. Further reading and resources are listed in the References.

Notes

1. See: *http://www.wipo.int/about-wipo/en/overview.html*

2. See American Library Association (ALA): *http://www.ala.org/ala/washoff/WOissues/copyrightb/distanceed/distanceeducation.htm*

3. See: *http://www.hmso.gov.uk/*

4. See: *http://www.austlii.edu.au/au/legis/cth/consol_act/ca1968133/*

5. Statutory Instrument 2003 No. 2498: The Copyright and Related Rights Regulations 2003. Available online at: *http://www.legislation.hmso.gov.uk/si/si2003/20032498.htm*

6. See: *http://www.ala.org/ala/acrl/acrlpubs/whitepapers/statementfair.htm*

7. Stanford University Library. Copyright and Fair Use: *http://fairuse.stanford.edu/index.html*

8. More information about this study is available on the JISC website: *http://www.jisc.ac.uk/index.cfm?name=prog_middss_studies* and also from Intralect, the company undertaking the study: *http://www.intrallect.com/drm-study/*

9. SURF is the Dutch higher education and research partnership organisation for network services and information and communications technology (ICT). More information is available at: *http://www.surf.nl/en/*

10. Amazon (2004), Conditions of Use. Available at: *http://www.amazon.co.uk/exec/obidos/tg/browse/-/1040616/ref=cs_hd_lp_22/202-2461530-9615817*. Accessed February 2004.

11. See: *http://www.freeimages.co.uk/terms.htm*

12. See: *http://creativecommons.org/*

13. See: *http://www.intrallect.com/drm-study/*

14. See: *http://library.curtin.edu.au/copyright/copybystaff.html*

15. See: *http://www.libraries.psu.edu/mtss/copyright.html*

16. See: *http://teaching.lse.ac.uk/tech/copyright/*

17. For more information about this project see: *http://www.ucl.ac.uk/epd/tqef/core/*

18. See: *http://www.ucl.ac.uk*

19. See: *http://www.derby.ac.uk/*

20. See: *http://www.cla.co.uk*

21. See: *http://www.copyright.com*

22. See: *http://www.copyright.com.au/*

References

Australian Copyright Council (2003) *Libraries: Managing Digital Resources*. Redfern, NSW: Australian Copyright Council.

Bide, M., Oppenheim, C. and Ramsden, A. (1997) *Charging mechanism for digitized texts: 2nd supporting study for the JISC/PA*. JISC. Available from: *http://www.ukoln.ac.uk/services/elib/papers/pa/charging/*.

Bruwelheid, Janis (1995) *The Copyright Primer for Librarians and Educators*. American Library Association

Cornish, Graham (2001) *Copyright: Interpreting the Law for Libraries and Educators*, 3rd edn. London: Library Association.

Crews, Kenneth D. (2000) *Copyright Essentials for Librarians and Educators*. ALA Editions.

Goldstein, Paul (2001) *International Copyright: Principles, Law, and Practice*. Oxford: Oxford University Press.

Harris, Lesley Ellen (2002) *Licensing Digital Content: A Practical Guide for Librarians*. ALA Editions.

Hoffmann, Gretchen McCord (2001) *Copyright in Cyberspace: Questions and Answers for Librarians*. Neal-Schuman Publishers.

JISC/SURF (2004) *Copyright Doesn't Stop at the Border: SURF Foundation and JISC to combine forces*. Press release, 25 June. Utrecht: JISC/SURF. Available online at: *http://www.surf.nl/download/0408%20Press%20release%20JISC%20-%20SURF.pdf*.

Johnston, Wanda K. and Roark, Derrie B. (1996) *A Copyright Sampler*. American Library Association

Norman, Sandy (2004) *Practical Copyright for Information Professionals: The CILIP Handbook*. London: Facet Publishing.

Pedley, Paul (2000) *Copyright for Library and Information Service Professionals*, 2nd edn. London: Aslib.

5

Technical standards, specifications and access management

Introduction

Since the first computer-based library systems in the 1960s, librarians have had to work increasingly closely with technologists and computer scientists. Systems librarians often have an extensive knowledge of technical issues; however, this book is not aimed at the technologically savvy librarian. It is aimed at the regular information professional who wants to keep up with the times and be able to hold their own in a fast-changing world.

An ever-increasing amount of jargon exists in the world of digital libraries and virtual learning environments. This chapter attempts to cut through the jargon, to define the key terms that you really need to know about and to give you a working knowledge of other terms that you might hear. It is written in plain English and should enable you to hold your own in most conversations with technical staff. It is worth remembering that learning technology is a relatively new field and staff in this area love acronyms and jargon. Most of these terms are really just long words for very simple concepts. So don't be put off, and don't forget, if you can learn the Dewey Decimal Classification and MARC then you are well on your way! This chapter is designed to be a quick reference guide to cover most of the technological language associated with virtual learning environments and electronic resources. General standards and specifications are first discussed. The chapter then goes on to examine standards in the library professions and standards and specifications in the e-learning sector.

What are standards and why are they important?

Technical standards are important because of the rapid pace of technological change. In the library world, the use of standards in all sorts of areas is well established and their importance widely recognised. However, in the e-learning sphere, standards are only beginning to be established. The key word here is interoperability. Without standards, information can become 'locked' into proprietary solutions. This means that your data can only be retrieved or transformed with difficulty. Proprietary solutions are everywhere; for example, in libraries we rely on commercial vendors to supply many library management systems. However, it is important that these solutions conform to recognised standards, so that we are not tied to one library management system forever. The same is true with e-learning systems and many of the associated technologies.

The World Wide Web: from HTML to XML

It seems hard to believe that the World Wide Web is only a little over ten years old. It was invented in 1991 by a computer scientist called Tim Berners-Lee. Berners-Lee created the first web page using HyperText Mark-up Language (HTML) and put it online in August of that year. In 1994 Berners Lee went on to found the World Wide Web Consortium (W3C) at the Massachusetts Institute for Technology in the US. The Consortium establishes standards for the World Wide Web. In 2003, they decided that all standards must contain royalty-free technology, so they can be easily adopted by anyone.

Some librarians have become familiar with HTML, although knowledge of this language is not essential to create web pages. Most modern web browsers now come with HTML composition tools that allow users to create web pages with little or no knowledge of this language. These tools use WYSIWYG (what you see is what you get) and examples of such packages are Microsoft Frontpage or Netscape Composer. For more sophisticated web page creation the Macromedia package, Dreamweaver, has greater potential for the more experienced designer, but can also be used in a relatively simplistic way with minimal training.

In the real world, computer systems and databases frequently contain data in incompatible formats. One of the most time-consuming challenges for developers has been to exchange data between such systems over the Internet. XML (eXtensible Mark-up Language) is a language that is being increasingly used for web publishing and has been a recommendation of the World Wide Web Consortium (W3C: *http://www.w3.org/*) since 1996. XML is a 'neutral' format designed to describe the structure of data, while HTML focuses on its presentation. XML needs to be transformed into HTML (or XHTML) to display it in a web browser. XML is particularly useful for publishing data that are structured, for example a reading list, or a collection of catalogue records.

To function effectively an XML document needs to conform to a set of rules laid down in a Document Type Definition (DTD). A DTD defines the relationships between legal tagged 'elements' or building blocks of an XML document. XML documents need to be 'validated' using parsing software, which checks them against the DTD to ensure that the element tags are used correctly and they are 'well formed'. A newer standard to emerge as a W3C recommendation is the XML Schema. Schemas are like DTDs but are written using XML syntax and allow greater flexibility. Anybody can create their own mark-up vocabulary, so the structure is intelligible to anyone else who consults the DTD or Schema.

XML and DTD are increasingly being used in the publishing and library communities. For example, they are being used by the National Library of Medicine which has created a free digital archive of biomedical and life sciences journal literature known as PubMed Central (*http://www.pubmedcentral.nih.gov/*). PubMed Central was launched in 2000 and provides free or open access to full-text journal articles, sometimes on a delayed basis. Journal publishers are encouraged to submit their material to PubMed Central as it provides a permanent and freely accessible archive at almost no cost to the publisher. The National Center for Biotechnology Information (NCBI), a centre of the National Library of Medicine (NLM), created the Journal Publishing DTD with the intention of providing a common format for the creation of journal content in XML. Publishers are encouraged to submit their material in either SGML format or XML format, or to use the DTD to define the incoming data. The DTD was created from the Journal Archiving and Interchange DTD Suite. The DTD Suite is a series of XML modules that define elements and attributes that describe the textual and graphical content of journal articles. In addition, the Journal Archiving and Interchange DTD Suite describes some non-article material such as letters, editorials and book reviews.

Style sheets are an important development in web technology and they can be used with both HTML and XML. Rather than using HTML to determine the appearance of a web publication, the rules governing presentation can be encoded into a style sheet. Applying a new style sheet can change the appearance of a publication dramatically, even though the information remains the same. XML style sheets use eXtensible Style Language (XSL), which is used to create XSLTs that transform XML documents into other formats like XHTML. Style sheets used with HTML documents are typically in Cascading Style Sheet (CSS) format.

An excellent guide to XML for librarians has recently been published by Gilmour (2003), which provides an introduction to the topic and explains the relevance of XML to librarianship. In areas such as cataloguing and classification, XML is becoming increasingly important, because it provides a way to share and exchange information. Some practical projects using XML in libraries are described by Banerjee (2002). For example, in 1993, the library at the University of California–Berkeley began developing a method for encoding archival materials in XML. The project led to the development of the Encoded Archival Description (EAD) standard, which is now maintained by the Library of Congress. Banerjee also describes how Washington Research Library Consortium is using XML to provide access to electronic resources through a system known as ALADIN (Access to Library and Database Information Network). Finally he describes how the Library of Congress, in spring 2002, produced an official specification for representing MARC data in XML format. He argues that XML will have a greater impact on the work of libraries in the future and that the:

> ... simplicity and flexibility of XML make it possible to integrate services and resources in ways that would have been impossible just a few years ago. Vendors, libraries, and open source programmers are all interested in finding ways to search many kinds of resources with a single query, and XML represents a major step forward in making this goal a reality. (Banerjee, 2002, p. 35)

Another term you may hear used is Standard Generalised Mark-up Language (SGML). This is the oldest of the mark-up languages and became an international standard in 1986 (ISO 8879, 1986). XML is derived from SGML, and also provides a set of rules in a DTD to describe the structure of an electronic document.

Metadata and standards

Following the proliferation of the World Wide Web in the mid-1990s everyone suddenly started talking about metadata. Metadata has been described as 'data about data', or the electronic equivalent of the library catalogue record. However, Chowdhury (2003, p. 138) argued that this definition does not say anything about the purpose of metadata and suggested three definitions from other authors, including:

- 'Data which describes attributes of a resource' (Dempsey and Heery, 1997);

- 'Meaningful data describing another discrete data object' (Gill, 1998, p. 9);

- 'Data associated with objects which relieves their potential users of having to have full advance knowledge of their existence or characteristics' (Dempsey and Heery, 1998, p. 149).

Metadata is used to facilitate the use of digital objects in a networked environment.

Dublin Core

Dublin Core is a term that you are probably familiar with as it's been around for a while now. The key thing to remember here is that it's Dublin, Ohio, not Dublin, Ireland! Dublin Core is a metadata standard devised in 1995 by a group of librarians, digital library researchers and technical experts and coordinated by OCLC. The organisation is known as the Dublin Core Metadata Initiative (DCMI) and everything you might want to know can be found from its website.[1] It has a large number of working groups and members include the Library of Congress, JISC, the national libraries of Germany, Canada and Australia, to name but a few. Its mission is defined as follows.

> ... to make it easier to find resources using the Internet through the following activities:
> (1) Developing metadata standards for discovery across domains,
> (2) Defining frameworks for the interoperation of metadata sets, and,
> (3) Facilitating the development of community- or disciplinary-specific metadata sets that are consistent with items 1 and 2.[2]

What exactly is Dublin Core and what does it mean to everyday librarians? Dublin Core is a set of metadata standards used to describe electronic resources. It has 15 elements covering a document's title, subject and coverage, intellectual property (e.g. creator and the associated rights) and instantiation, such as the date, format or language. You can check if a website has Dublin Core metadata by viewing the HTML source. Surveys suggest that few websites currently use Dublin Core. While librarians have been talking about the importance of metadata standards, there is a very real issue of who creates metadata, and whether web authors are the right people to be 'cataloguing' their resources. Caplan (2003) has provided a detailed overview of the metadata landscape, written specifically for librarians.

The Semantic Web

The Semantic Web is the current project of Tim Berners-Lee, which aims to develop standards and tools that allow meaning to be added to the content of web pages. It is a collaborative effort led by the W3C, with participation from a large number of researchers and industrial partners.[3] HTML does not describe or categorise the contents of web pages. The Semantic Web will address this issue by allowing content to be classified in XML documents using various languages. These languages include:

- Resource Description Framework (RDF) – a 1999 W3C recommendation that provided a lightweight ontology system to support the exchange of knowledge on the Web;
- Topic Maps, developed by the ISO (the International Organisation for Standardisation) and IEC (the International Electrotechnical Commission) – topic maps are abstract structures that can encode knowledge and connect this encoded knowledge to relevant information resources;
- Web Ontology Language (OWL) – a 2004 W3C recommendation for publishing and sharing data using ontologies (or conceptual schema) on the Internet.

The Semantic Web is very much in its infancy, but promises to give meaning to information on the Internet. It is not a separate web, but an extension of the current one:

> The Semantic Web will bring structure to the meaningful content of Web pages, creating an environment where software agents roaming from page to page can readily carry out sophisticated tasks for users. (Berners-Lee et al., 2001)

The Semantic Web is a development that is currently being led by computer scientists, but one where the skills of librarians in creating taxonomies and ontologies will be invaluable. Lougee (2002), in her book examining emerging roles for the research library in the digital age, recognises that librarians have the potential to contribute significantly to this effort. Meanwhile, Sadeh and Walker (2003) consider how library portals, which offer cross searching of heterogeneous resources, are still facing challenges which may well be addressed by developments towards the Semantic Web. While such developments may seem futuristic, they may very soon be a reality and the Semantic Web is an area of emerging standards from which librarians can learn and to which they can contribute.

Open source solutions

The Open Source Initiative (OSI) originated in the late 1990s and is a not-for-profit corporation that manages and promotes what is known as the Open Source Definition. The definition specifies that software must be distributed according to a set of criteria, including: that the software is freely distributed, that the source code is also supplied and that modifications can be made to the code. Open source not only has the advantage of being free, but arguably the software is more responsive to the needs of users, with quality rather than profit driving the developers. Software peer review is also widely encouraged, which in a similar way to peer review in the academic sense bestows a level of validity on the work. The most famous product is probably the open source operating system, LINUX. Others include the Apache web server and MySQL database.

Open source products exist in both the library community and the e-learning sector. Chudnov (1999) described how open source could provide the future of library systems. He cites advantages such as reduced costs, not being locked into a single vendor, and how the community can work together to solve accessibility issues. Some open source library products include Koha,[4] a New Zealand system which describes itself as the first open source integrated library system. Koha is being used in several public libraries in New Zealand, Nelsonville Public Library in Ohio and a school library in Canada. Greenstone[5] is an open-source digital library system, again originating in New Zealand at the University of Waikato, although it was also developed in cooperation with UNESCO. This system is used by over 20 institutions to facilitate access to digital library collections, including Project Gutenberg,[6] the

Indian Institute of Science Publications Database[7] and Gresham College Archive[8] in London.

Another open source library product is MyLibrary[9] which is described as a library portal (see Chapter 1 for more details). MyLibrary defines itself as:

> ... a user-driven, customizable interface to collections of Internet resources – a portal. Primarily designed for libraries, the system's purpose is to reduce information overload by allowing patrons to select as little or as much information as they so desire for their personal pages.

MyLibrary was created as part of the Digital Library Initiatives at North Carolina State University (NCSU) and users can create an account on the system to gain personalised access to the library's resources.

In the e-learning sector there are a large number of open source virtual learning environments that are available to download. Several universities have opted to develop their own VLE in-house and often these products are available as open source. Other institutions have rarely adopted these systems although the originating institution uses them successfully. Open source VLEs include the Bodington,[10] which was developed at the University of Leeds and is now also being used at the University of Oxford. UCLA developed Classweb[11] in 1997 and currently runs over 300 classes on the system each quarter. Another open source VLE that has been attracting attention recently is Moodle.[12] Martin Dougiamas, a web developer at Curtin University of Technology who was frustrated with the capabilities of commercial VLE software, developed Moodle. The software 'supports a social constructionist pedagogy' which has at its heart communication, collaboration and critical reflection.

One of the biggest drawbacks to open source systems is the staff time and resources that are required to support such initiatives. This has meant that many libraries choose to buy off-the-shelf library management products. Similarly, commercial e-learning solutions are used more frequently than open-source products.

Library standards

Many standards in the library community are developed and endorsed by the National Information Standards Organisation (NISO) in the United States. The organisation describes itself as:

... a non-profit association accredited by the American National Standards Institute (ANSI), [that] identifies, develops, maintains, and publishes technical standards to manage information in our changing and ever-more digital environment.[13]

NISO have developed over 30 standards of importance to the library profession, in diverse areas such as information retrieval, library management, preservation and storage, and publishing and information management.

Cross searching: Z39.50 to MetaLib

One of the first areas where interoperability and standards were required was in the field of information retrieval and specifically library catalogues or OPACs. The Information Retrieval (Z39.50) Application Service Definition and Protocol Specification was an important development and is discussed by Lynch (1997) who provides an overview of developments since the 1970s. He defines Z39.50 as:

... a protocol which specifies data structures and interchange rules that allow a client machine (called an 'origin' in the standard) to search databases on a server machine (called a 'target' in the standard) and retrieve records that are identified as a result of such a search.

Z39.50 facilitates cross searching of resources and the construction of union catalogues, which was an important feature of many of the eLib Projects. Z39.50 refers its NISO standard number, and it has also become an international standard with ISO number 23950.

The vast majority of modern library management systems comply with the Z39.50 standard. The standard is one of the core technologies at the heart of portal developments that is leading to an increasing overlap between e-learning solutions and digital libraries. Cross searching of a variety of electronic resources in addition to the library catalogue is now possible with library portal technology. Various commercial library management systems offer portal products, including MetaLib[14] from ExLibris, ENCompass[15] from Endeavor and ZPortal[16] from Fretwell-Downing to name but a few. There are also a number of open source solutions, such as MyLibrary, that were discussed earlier in this chapter. A review of library portals was undertaken by Cox and Yeates (2002) who state:

> Z39.50 and Dublin Core are the core underlying standards/technologies in use ... we see this increasingly being superseded by XML (XPath, XML Query, XQuery, XSLT) and the notion of web services. (Cox and Yeates, 2002, p. 4)

Boss (2002) maintains that most portals have the following features: intuitive and customisable web interface, personalised content presentation, security and communication and collaboration tools.[17] Cox (2003) argues that the core function of portals is the cross searching of resources and providing the appropriate copy of resources using OpenURL (this is discussed later in this chapter). JISC recently funded a project to examine the implementation of one library portal at Loughborough University (Hamblin and Stubbings, 2003). The project found that the portal led to a dramatic increase in the use of electronic databases. In any case, there are obvious overlaps between library portals and virtual learning environments and the importance of a library portal interacting with the VLE is paramount:

> This could mean somehow offering management services to resources embedded in course materials. For example, such systems might be used to manage readings lists or collections of relevant resources that would be viewed through the VLE. (Cox and Yeates, 2002, p. 9)

Electronic journals and standards

There is in general a lack of specifically targeted standards for e-journals, although a number of technical standards are having an impact on their publication and on access to them. Standards in areas such as metadata, identifiers and traditional cataloguing are becoming important, with three emerging standards: OpenURL and DOI (Digital Object Identifier) to facilitate reference linking, and ONIX for Serials, a metadata standard, to support business applications in the serials publication sector. Perhaps one of the greatest challenges presented by electronic journals is also maintaining up-to-date title and subject lists of resources and locating appropriate copies of an item. Many new e-journal solutions have therefore come onto the market, including products such as SFX, Xrefer and Serials Solution.

Journal articles are identified as discrete 'digital objects' and there is a number of relevant recent standards for identifying digital and other objects. These include SICI (Serial Item and Contribution Identifier) code and DOI. Schemes for persistent names for Internet addresses have also been developed, most notably OCLC's PURL (Persistent URL) system, CNRI's Handles and the OpenURL.

OpenURL, SICI and Digital Object Identifiers (DOI)

The OpenURL standard was developed by the library management system supplier Ex-Libris and released as a draft standard for trial use in April 2003 by the National Information Standards Organisation (NISO). It enables a user who has retrieved an article citation to obtain immediate access to the 'most appropriate' copy of that object through the implementation of extended linking services. The selection of the best copy is based on user and organisational preferences regarding the location of the copy, its cost, agreements with information suppliers and similar considerations. This selection occurs without the knowledge of the user; it is made possible by the transport of metadata with the OpenURL link from the source citation to a 'resolver' (the link server), which stores the preference information and the links to the appropriate copy of the material.

Serial Item and Contribution Identifier (SICI) is another standard which can be used as an article level identifier. SICI is an ANSI/NISO standard that was developed to uniquely identify serial items, typically issues, and their contributions, typically articles.[18]

A digital object identifier (or DOI) is a permanent identifier given to a World Wide Web file or other Internet document so that if its Internet address changes, users will be redirected to its new address. DOIs need to be submitted to a centrally managed directory, and to access a document users enter the address of that directory plus the DOI into their browser instead of a regular Internet address. The Association of American Publishers in partnership with the Corporation for National Research Initiatives founded the system, but it is now administered by the International DOI Foundation. An example of its implementation is CrossRef, the DOI agency providing services to science, technology and medicine publishers, by which researchers can link directly from bibliographic reference lists to source publications. The European Union announced in August 2004 that DOIs will be assigned to all of its publications.

Open Archives Initiative (OAI)

An important development that has its roots in the development of e-print archives is the Open Archives Initiative (OAI).[19] The OAI develops and promotes interoperability standards that aim to facilitate the efficient dissemination of content. Its work is supported by the Digital Library Federation, the Coalition for Networked Information and the National Science Foundation. A key development is the Open Archives Initiative Protocol for Metadata Harvesting (OAI-PMH), which defines a mechanism for harvesting records containing metadata from repositories. Many communities are beginning to or potentially could benefit from the open archives approach. The Internet and the growth of information in digital format have broadened the potential clientele of many repositories of information.

Middleware

Middleware is a term used increasingly frequently both in the library and the e-learning sector. Middleware has been described as the 'glue' between the network and applications. For example, some middleware products link a database system to a web server. This allows users to request data from the database using forms displayed on a web browser, and it enables the web server to return dynamic web pages based on the user's requests and profile.

Standards in the e-learning sector

In the UK, CETIS (the Centre for Educational Technology Interoperability Standards) 'represents UK higher and further education on international educational standards initiatives.'[20] Their website has a large amount of information about interoperability standards. The site also offers news about the latest happenings in the field, feature articles and a collection of short pieces about the different standards. There are also introductory essays; if you are new to interoperability standards there is an excellent reference section which defines many of the key acronyms and terms you will hear.

IMS

The IMS Global Learning Consortium develops and promotes the adoption of open technical specifications for interoperable learning technology. Several IMS specifications have become worldwide de facto standards for delivering learning products and services. IMS specifications and related publications are made available to the public at no charge from their website (*http://www.imsglobal.org*). No fee is required to implement the specifications.

More recently, other bodies have become involved in learning technology standards. These include the Institute of Electrical and Electronics Engineers (IEEE), ISO and the European CEN/ISSS and Prometheus initiatives. There are also other bodies that are involved, including the American Aircraft Industry (AICC), and the US Department of Defense's Advanced Distributed Learning programme (ADL). These groups are committed to collaboration to achieve the goal of establishing learning technology interoperability standards.

SCORM (shareable courseware object reference model)

SCORM is a set of technical standards that enable web-based learning systems to find, import, share, reuse and export learning content in a standardised way. It is written primarily for vendors who build learning management systems and learning content authoring tools so they know what they need to do to their products to conform with SCORM technically.

Learning Object Metadata (LOM)

Learning Object Metadata or LOM is a metadata schema for describing learning objects, or learning resources from the Institute of Electrical and Electronics Engineers (IEEE). The IEEE provides a wide variety of e-learning and other specifications, almost all of them very particularly focused on issues of technical interoperability. The IEEE LOM standard has received widespread support from the educational technology industry and it has also been adopted by many publicly funded projects. The specification has, at its heart, the desire to construct reusable learning objects, that can then be made accessible through digital repositories.

The LOM specification is being used by several international repository projects. A key example is MERLOT (Multimedia Educational Resource for Learning and Online Teaching) (*http://www .merlot.org/*) which contains a wealth of reusable online learning materials. The LOM specification is also being used by ARIADNE, the digital repository funded by the European Union (*http://www.ariadne-eu.org/*) and the US Department of Defense SCORM initiative (*http://www.adlnet.org/*). In the UK, the JORUM + Project is another example of a digital repository using this specification. The project is funded by JISC and runs from 2002 until 2005. It seeks to provide a learning object repository for further and higher education to encourage and facilitate the deposit, reuse and sharing of learning materials in UK tertiary education. A scoping study was undertaken in 2003 to investigate the requirements of the community for such a repository. JISC recognises the importance of such repositories and maintains that:

> Learning object repositories can provide access to a wide range of learning materials for students and lecturers and also minimize the need to reinvent the wheel across different institutions or subject areas.[21]

The LOM standard defines approximately 80 separate 'elements' for the description and management of learning resources. These include generic items such as title, author, description and keywords, technical aspects such as file size and type, and also include educational and interpretive aspects like 'typical learning time' or 'educational context'.

Resource list interoperability

Throughout this book we have seen how digital libraries and e-learning systems are moving closer together. In the area of standards, however, this movement has been slower, with library standards being developed by NISO and e-learning standards by IMS. Nevertheless, following the JISC-funded DiVLE Programme, which was discussed in some detail in Chapter 2, IMS began work on a standard for resource list interoperability. In June 2003 IMS published a Charter for Resource List Interoperability which is available on the Internet.[22] The consortium recognised that there was currently no metadata standard for the description of resources associated with courses within virtual learning environments. Consequently, resources lists were often created by relying on ad hoc or proprietary methods and tools. IMS are currently working to establish specifications for the exchange of structured metadata between systems that provide resources and those that harvest and organise those resources for pedagogic purposes.

Access management standards

One of the big technical issues associated with electronic resources and virtual learning environments is authentication (i.e. identifying the persons attempting to gain access to electronic resources) and authorisation (determining from that person's identity, and often using other sources of information, what privileges the individual has and hence whether access should be allowed or not). Many electronic library resources and almost all virtual learning environments need access management for security reasons, to ensure the systems and resources are only accessed by designated users. JISC have invested a large amount of funding into this area, most recently through their Authentication, Authorisation and Accounting (AAA) Programme.[23] In recognition that international standards are emerging in the area, the UK has been working with other countries to facilitate these developments. They also have a programme of research projects which are scheduled to report at the end of 2004.

Electronic resources and access management

Until recently, authentication to electronic resources was through IP address, therefore only those users accessing a resource from within the IP range of an institution, typically from within a university campus, could gain access. However, this method has a number of inherent weaknesses, nor does it allow for distance learning and the increasing need for remote access to resources. The solution to this problem is to provide access to resources via a proxy server. This means that users connect remotely to the proxy server and would then appear to be within the campus, so could gain access to resources. This method of access management is currently used in most US universities, e.g. Princeton University, Northwestern University and UC Berkeley.

The UK developed a system to address this problem of off-campus access through the Athens Access Management system. Developed in 1996 by Eduserv it is currently established as the de facto standard for secure access management to web-based services for the UK education and health sectors. In 2000 JISC awarded Athens the contract for the Provision of Authentication Services for UK higher and further education until 2006. All members of the institution have an Athens password through which they can access remotely a range of electronic resources.

Other access management systems include: PAPI (Point of Access to Information Providers), developed by the Spanish National Research Network (RedIRIS); Akenti[24] which was developed by the US Department of Energy; and PERMIS (PrivilEge and Role Management Infrastructure Standards Validation) which was funded by the European Commission under their Information Society Initiative in Standardization (ISI) Programme.

In the US, developments in this area are being led by Internet2[25] which is a consortium led by 206 universities, working in partnership with industry and government. The consortium is 'seeking to develop and deploy advanced network applications and technologies, accelerating the creation of tomorrow's Internet.' The group have developed a middleware solution known as Shibboleth, which is currently on trial in the UK as a potential replacement for the Athens system. Shibboleth is a federated system of authentication and authorisation and has been described by Carmody (2001) as:

> ... investigating architectures, frameworks, and practical technologies to support inter-institutional sharing and controlled access to web available services.[26]

Shibboleth is open source and standards based.

There is also considerable research in the area of digital certificates, which are based on the Public/Private Key technology. Digital certificates are an important means for authentication that are more secure than usernames and passwords. Again the development of standards in this area is important and the most common type is the X.509 v3 certificate, which was proposed as a standard by the Internet Engineering Task Force (IETF).[27] The system was developed to protect nuclear missiles and each key has been described as a unique encryption device. No two keys are ever identical, which is why a key can be used to identify its owner. The keys always work in pairs and information encrypted by the public key can only be decrypted by the corresponding private key. Public keys can be freely distributed, but a private key is kept secure, usually on your own computer. A digital certificate automates the distribution of private keys so that when you install a digital certificate on your computer, you obtain a private key. Digital certificates are particularly important in the e-commerce sector; however, they have also been investigated by the JISC-funded project, Digital Certificate Operation in a Complex Environment (DCOCE)[28] based at the University of Oxford.

Access management and VLEs

Access to virtual learning environments is typically integrated with student records systems and network usernames and passwords, so for example students would gain access to WebCT using their network user name and password. This area has been much enhanced by the development of standards.

LDAP is another standard that you will hear mentioned in the context of VLEs. It stands for Lightweight Directory Access Protocol and is an Internet protocol that e-mail programs use to look up contact information from a server. This standard has a number of functions, including allowing an organisation to keep an up-to-date e-mail directory. Software companies such as Microsoft, IBM, Lotus and Netscape adopted this standard. LDAP servers also provide 'authentication' services, so that web, e-mail and file-sharing servers, for example, can use a single list of authorised users and passwords. By using LDAP, a university can ensure that network usernames and passwords remain synchronised.

Conclusion

This chapter has looked at many technical standards and specifications associated with electronic resources and virtual learning environments. It is designed to provide a very brief overview of many of the major concepts and standards, therefore the further reading suggested at the end of the book is particularly useful in this chapter. It is inevitable that library databases and e-learning systems contain data in incompatible formats. Therefore one of the most time-consuming challenges for developers has been to exchange data between such systems over the Internet, and standards that allow interoperability are an extremely important goal for the librarian, the learning technologist and the systems engineer.

Notes

1. See: *http://dublincore.org/*

2. See: *http://dublincore.org/about/*

3. More information is available at: *http://www.w3.org/2001/sw/*

4. See: *http://www.koha.org/*

5. See: *http://www.greenstone.org/*

6. See: *http://public.ibiblio.org/gsdl/cgi-bin/library?a=p&p=about&c=gberg*

7. See: *http://vidya-mapak.ncsi.iisc.ernet.in/cgi-bin/library*

8. See: *http://www.gresham.ac.uk/greenstone/frameset.html*

9. See: *http://dewey.library.nd.edu/mylibrary/*

10. See: *http://bodington.org/index.html*

11. See: *http://classweb.ucla.edu/*

12. See: *http://moodle.com/*

13. See: *http://www.niso.org/about/index.html*

14. See: *http://www.exlibrisgroup.com/metalib.htm*

15. See: *http://encompass.endinfosys.com/*

16. See: *http://www.fdusa.com/products/zportal.html*

17. See: *http://www.ala.org/ala/pla/plapubs/technotes/librarywebportals.htm*

18. More information about SICI is available from: *http://sunsite.Berkeley .EDU/SICI/*

19. See: *http://www.openarchives.org/*

20. See: *http://www.cetis.ac.uk/*

21. JORUM Scoping and Technical Appraisal Study, Volume I: Overview and Recommendations, p. 3. Available from: *http://www.jorum.ac.uk/vol1_ fin.pdf*

22. See: *http://imsglobal.org/rliCharter.pdf*

23. See: *http://www.jisc.ac.uk/index.cfm?name=programme_aaa*

24. See: *http://www-itg.lbl.gov/security/Akenti/homepage.html*

25. See: *http://www.internet2.edu/*

26. Carmody, Steven, *Shibboleth Overview and Requirements*, Shibboleth Working Group Document, 20 February 2001. Available from *http:// shibboleth.internet2.edu/docs/draft-internet2-shibboleth-requirements-01.html*

27. See: *http://www.ietf.org/*

28. See: *http://www.dcoce.ox.ac.uk/*

References

Banerjee, Kyle (2002) 'How does XML help libraries?', *Computers in Libraries*, 22(8), 30–5. Available from: *http://www.infotoday.com/cilmag/sep02/Banerjee.htm*.

Berners-Lee, T., Hendler, J. and Lassila, O. (2001) 'The Semantic Web', *Scientific American*, May. Available from: *http://www.scientificamerican.com/article.cfm?articleID=00048144-10D2-1C70-84A9809EC588EF21&pageNumber=2&catID=2*.

Boss, R. W. (2002) 'How to plan and implement a library portal', *Library Technology Reports*, 38(6), 1–54.

Caplan, Priscilla (2003) *Metadata Fundamentals for All Librarians*. American Library Association Editions.

Centre for Educational Technology Interoperability Standards (CETIS) (2004) *CETIS Reference*. Available from: *http://www.cetis.ac.uk/encyclopedia*.

Chowdhury, G. G. and Chowdhury, S. (2003) *Introduction to Digital Libraries*. London: Facet Publishers.

Chudnov, Daniel (1999) 'Open source software: the future of library systems', *Library Journal*, 124(13): 40–3.

Cox, A. (2003) 'Choosing a library portal system', *VINE: The Journal of Information and Knowledge Management Systems*, 33(1), 37–41.

Cox, A. and Yeates, R. (2002) *Library-Oriented Portals Solutions*, Techwatch Report TSW 02-03. London: JISC.

Dempsey, L. and Heery, R. (1997) *A review of metadata: a survey of current resource description formats*, March. Available from: *http://www.ukoln.ac.uk/metadata/DESIRE/overview/*.

Gill, T. (1998) 'Metadata and the World Wide Web', in M. Baca (ed.), *Introduction to Metadata: Pathways to Digital Information*. Available from *http://www.getty.edu/research/institute/standards/intro/metadata/2_articles/gill/*.

Gilmour, Ron (2003) *XML: a guide for librarians*. LITA Guide, 11.

Hamblin, Y. and Stubbings, R. (2003) *The implementation of MetaLib and SFX at Loughborough University Library: a case study*. Available from: *http://www.jisc.ac.uk/uploaded_documents/Metalibcasestudy.doc*.

Lougee, W. P. (2002) *Diffuse libraries: emergent roles for the research library in the digital age*. Washington, DC: CLIR. Available from: *http://www.clir.org/pubs/abstract/pub108abst.html*.

Lynch, Clifford A. (1997) 'The Z39.50 information retrieval standard: part I: a strategic view of its past, present and future', *D-lib magazine* (April). Available from: *http://www.dlib.org/dlib/april97/04lynch.html*.

Sadeh, T. and Walker, J. (2003) 'Library portals: toward the semantic web', *New Library World*, 104(1184/1185), 11–19.

6

Case studies and practical examples

Introduction

The purpose of this final chapter is to provide a number of case studies that highlight ways in which electronic resources and digital libraries can be integrated. The four case studies are all from higher education institutions within the UK and include:

- the use of digitised core readings or electronic course packs within a virtual learning environment;
- the use of a reading list management system with a description of how this is presented in the virtual learning environment;
- the creation of a 'library area' within a virtual learning environment, based on a model developed as part of a JISC-funded project;
- the creation of an information literacy course for students, delivered via the virtual learning environment.

There is no standard format used in the case studies and they vary in length and approach. However, they illustrate ways in which librarians are working with learning technologists and techniques for integrating systems to improve the learning experience.

The last section of this chapter is a practical guide to creating links to different electronic journal resources. These links can then be added to online reading lists, lecture notes or even teachers' personal websites. The ability to link to these resources ensures that learners are able to locate the resources as they are situated in their learning space. It also means that the librarian can be sure their collections are being fully exploited by both teachers and learners.

Case study 1: Electronic coursepacks in the VLE

The London School of Economics and Political Science (LSE) is a world-class centre for research and teaching in the social sciences. Founded in 1895, it is renowned for its atmosphere of intellectual argument and debate. LSE graduates and former staff have included Nobel Prize winners in Economics, Peace or Literature, around 29 past or present Heads of State, 30 current UK MPs and 29 current peers of the House of Lords. Located in the heart of London it has close links with business, the media and government. The LSE has almost 7,000 full-time students and around 750 part-time students. Of these, 38 per cent come from the UK, 18 per cent from other European Union countries and 44 per cent from more than 120 countries worldwide. The LSE Library contains more than four million items, including Fabian, Liberal Party and other political archives and the famous Charles Booth 'poverty maps' of nineteenth-century London.

At the LSE, integration between the library and e-learning has been important for a number of years. This case study describes how the electronic coursepack service, which copyright clears and digitises core readings, became central to the work of the Centre for Learning Technology. It also examines how the service was established, how it currently operates and what the future might hold. Further expansion and developments to the service undoubtedly will be shaped by the move towards a blanket licence for digitisation in the UK, which seems likely to be in place by 2005.

Introduction and background

In 1999 the Library, IT Services and the Teaching and Learning Development Office collaborated to establish a Learning and Teaching Technology Group, using staff on secondment. The group introduced a virtual learning environment to the School and also supported a pilot service to provide digitised core reading materials. This group subsequently became the Centre for Learning Technology and the electronic coursepack service scaled up significantly between 2001 and 2004. This expansion was made possible by funding provided by the LSE to pay copyright clearance fees and staff to undertake the digitisation.

The LSE first launched a pilot electronic coursepack service in 1999 using Teaching Quality Enhancement Funding from the Higher

Education Funding Council for England and an internal grant from the School. The service was a joint initiative between the library and the newly established Learning and Teaching Technologies Group. The service was led and promoted by the Assistant Librarian (Learning Technology) and supported by a part-time library assistant, who undertook copyright clearance and scanned the material. In the first year approximately 20 readings were copyright cleared and scanned in-house and this service was expanded the following year. The majority of the readings were made available to students via an online reading list in WebCT.

In 2001 the LSE joined the HERON Service and the newly appointed full-time Assistant Librarian undertook a review to compare the service with the in-house production process. Two coursepacks were outsourced to HERON. The experience of using HERON in 2001/2 indicated that this service had a number of advantages, including providing high-quality digitised files, obtaining permission for a large number of items and providing valuable information and contacts through the HERON members area and user group. In 2002 LSE decided to outsource approximately 30 per cent of the electronic coursepack production to HERON. This allowed the service to scale up significantly at a time when the staffing levels for the service remained constant. Since this date, the LSE has continued to produce electronic coursepacks in-house and outsource to HERON. In 2003/4 over 900 digitised files were made available to students from over 70 WebCT courses at a cost of approximately £47,000.

Equipment and resources

When launching an electronic coursepack service there are considerable resource implications, both for the hardware and software required, but also for a budget to pay permission fees. The LSE invested in the following equipment:

- server to store the digital files;
- high-quality scanner with sheet feeder;
- PC with Adobe Acrobat, FTP software.

The electronic coursepack service also had a significant budget to pay copyright clearance fees. In 2003/4 this budget was increased to £47,000. This allowed approximately 900 readings to be made available to students in over 70 courses.

Staffing

The LSE showed considerable foresight in placing a librarian within the learning technology team in 1999. The Assistant Librarian (Learning Technology) has responsibility for digital copyright, managing the electronic course pack service and integrating library resources into the VLE. The service was also supported by a part-time library assistant post, which in 2003 was increased to two part-time posts. The assistants undertake much of the routine copyright clearance work, liaising with the Copyright Licensing Agency, and dealing with online permission requests for the Copyright Clearance Center. They also scan material, add copyright notices to the documents and upload them to the secure server. Meanwhile the Assistant Librarian did much of the promotion and publicity for the service, carried out an evaluation of the procedures and processes and liaised with academic staff.

Digital rights management

With the enormous growth in the demand for the electronic coursepack service in 2001, it became clear that the simple in-house built database, which was recording bibliographic information and details about the price and licence for each extract, needed major modifications. Staff at the LSE had become familiar with the online system HERONweb, which was used to enter bibliographical details and track progress of items processed by HERON. Information, such as when the clearance was submitted, the price that was paid and the status of an extract at any one time, was extremely valuable. However, keeping track of the large number of extracts being processed in house was more difficult. Therefore the LSE approached HERON about the possibilities of developing a system that could manage both the material produced in house and the HERON material. A number of meetings were held between staff at the LSE and the Technical Manager at HERON and a detailed specification was drawn up by the LSE. This ultimately led to the development of Packtracker, which was initially given a trial at the LSE but is now available as a commercial product.[1] Packtracker was extremely important in the expansion of the electronic coursepack system. The system has numerous features including:

- automated permission requests to the CLA and to publishers accepting e-mail and written permissions;
- extract tracking so the status of an item can be seen at a glance;

- scheduling functions that allow staff to see, for example: all items that need scanning, all items awaiting copyright clearance, all items completed and uploaded;
- a 'week' function that allows material to be processed according to when it is required in the academic year;
- licence information so that material can be removed once a permission has expired or uploaded once it has been granted;
- a clear audit trail so that invoices can be traced and budgets managed.

Production process

The CLA Higher Education Digitisation Licence is currently operating on a transactional basis, therefore all readings that are scanned for class use require copyright permission. Until 2001 all digital readings were copyright cleared and scanned in-house. However, in 2001, to cope with the increased demand for the service, the LSE decided to outsource approximately a quarter of their electronic coursepacks to the HERON Service. This meant that requests could be submitted to HERON via their online system HERONweb, and the material would be copyright cleared and digital files subsequently provided. Before 2001 the service had processed no more than 100 items in an academic year; however, in line with the increased demand for WebCT courses, staff requests for electronic coursepacks increased exponentially.

Figure 6.1 shows the production process of the electronic coursepack service in 2003/4.

It is worth noting at this stage that many academic staff at LSE employ course designers, who are often PhD students, to do much of the work in creating and updating the WebCT course and electronic coursepack. Course designers are currently paid from a grant administered by the CLT. However, all staff setting up an online course are offered an electronic coursepack. Staff then liaise with the Assistant Librarian over the contents of the pack before it is submitted to the team for processing.

The first stage is usually checking the list to ensure all the required information is present (see below for more details). Material is then submitted first to the CLA for clearance and if this fails to the CCC. Publishers are used as the third option, unless a reading is an 'author permission', where free permission will be requested from the publisher. Once copyright clearance has been obtained the reading can be scanned. The readings are scanned at a resolution of 200 dpi using Adobe Acrobat

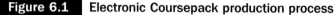

Figure 6.1 Electronic Coursepack production process

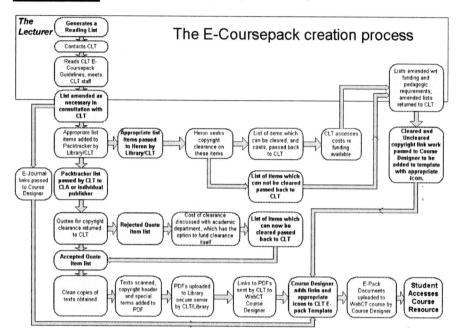

to create a PDF image file. All items then have a copyright header sheet inserted as the first page to comply with the CLA licence. This work is done in Acrobat, and the final file is saved locally on a PC before being uploaded to a secure server using FTP. The secure server is configured so that it uses IP authentication on-campus and the LSE network username and password for off-campus access. Each reading has a stable URL which is e-mailed to the lecturer and the course designer. They manually need to copy and paste the URL into the e-coursepack template file, then upload this to WebCT.

Requirements and limitations

To process the requests from academic staff for electronic coursepacks, a number of requirements and limitations were set up as the service became more established and demand increased. A limit on the number of items that could be submitted to the service was established in 2003, following some courses requesting over 90 core readings. The limit was set at 20 readings per term, or two readings per week. Readings were also expected to be no greater than 35 pages in length, which reduced the amount of printing that students needed to do and increased the likelihood of gaining copyright clearance. To speed up processing time for reading lists, staff were asked to supply the following information:

- course (module) title and code;
- lecturer(s) involved;
- estimated student numbers;
- full bibliographic details of the items they required;
- page numbers of the item they required;
- ISBN or ISSN;
- week of term reading was required;
- a clean photocopy of the item required.

Presenting the electronic coursepacks in WebCT

Until 2002, course designers were able to incorporate links to readings throughout a WebCT course. However, the Centre for Learning Technology (CLT) found that students had problems when links to electronic readings were presented without some indication of any access restrictions. They also found that the level of use for electronic readings (many of which have been copyright cleared or licensed specifically for a particular course) was dependent on how clear the links to readings were. Additionally, one of the biggest complaints from students regarding electronic readings were dead links, links that did not work off-campus and links that required a password. To overcome some of the problems students experienced, the CLT designed an online reading list template in HTML to incorporate reading materials that staff wished to distribute to students (see Figure 6.2). Course designers were automatically provided with a copy of the template in their WebCT designer file store. The template was designed to be used for:

- links to electronic journals;
- online sources;
- electronic coursepack readings;
- free electronic resources (websites) available on the Internet.

The template helped students to distinguish between electronic resources that require a subscription and are only available on the LSE campus and

Figure 6.2 Online reading list template being used to link to e-journals and electronic coursepacks

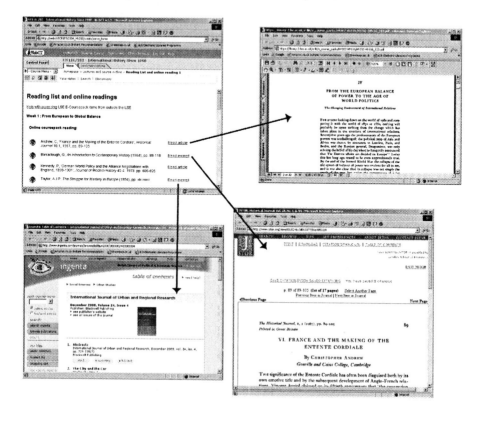

those resources that are freely available on the Internet. Two icons were devised to help to give a consistent look to electronic resources pages, which was particularly useful for students studying more than one course that uses WebCT. CLT also recommended that the template be placed in an obvious part of the course website, such as on the course home page, or within the 'content module' that often contains all the lecture material.

Several icons were developed as part of the template, as Figure 6.3 shows. An LSE icon was developed for readings that are only accessible on the LSE campus. This is used for e-journal links that are not available off campus. The globe icon is used for readings that are accessible on and off campus with or without a password, so it could be used for web links, electronic coursepacks or readings that have Athens authentication off campus.

Figure 6.3 The e-coursepack template in detail

Reading list and online readings

Help with accessing LSE E-Coursepack items from outside the LSE

Week 1 : From European to Global Balance
Content page body

Online coursepack reading:

Andrew, C, 'France and the Making of the Entente Cordiale', *Historical Journal* 10:1, 1967, pp. 89-105   Read article

Barraclough, G, *An Introduction to Contemporary History* (1964), pp. 88-118   Read excerpt

Kennedy, P, 'German World Policy and the Alliance Negotiations with England, 1898-1901', *Journal of Modern History* 45:4, 1973, pp. 605-625   Read article

Taylor, A J P, *The Struggle for Mastery in Europe* (1954), pp. xlx-xxxvi   Read excerpt

Williams, B, 'The Strategic Background to the Anglo-Russian Entente of August 1907', *Historical Journal* 9:3, 1966, pp. 360-373   Read article

Evaluation

Each year, as part of the student WebCT survey that is distributed by the CLT, feedback is obtained about the value of the electronic coursepack service. In 2003 focus groups were also held with students to further establish the value of online readings. The feedback has been overwhelmingly positive, with students maintaining that electronic coursepacks save them time hunting for material, make them more likely to carry out preparatory reading and solve the problem of providing large numbers of students with access to a core reading. Problems with the service usually arise when a reading cannot be made available for copyright reasons or when the link of the reading list is broken. Some students also complain about the costs associated with printing the material from the LSE campus printers, although the standard charge (5 pence per page) is levied for e-coursepacks and the readings can be printed for free from a home computer.

Problems and current issues

The major problems facing the service have been:

- high costs associated with digitisation with publishers charging per page, per student;
- the transactional nature of the CLA licence that requires all readings to be copyright cleared;

- the time taken to obtain copyright clearance;
- the need to renew licences for most material every year.

However, as discussed in Chapter 4, the Copyright Licensing Agency are reviewing the digitisation licence offered to the higher education community and moving towards a blanket licence that will cover both photocopying and scanning. This licence will be based on student numbers and, for an institution such as the LSE that is undertaking a large amount of digitisation, is likely to be highly cost effective. It will also reduce the administrative burden of the current system. Therefore the service is currently operating with the same budget as 2003/04 and will be reviewed following the launch of a new licence.

A second issue that will impact on the service is the launch of a reading list management system at the LSE. Following the DELIVER Project, Sentient Discover was purchased with the plan to roll it out over the next two years. This system has many advantages over the HTML-based templates that have been previously used.

Conclusion

It is clear that the electronic coursepack service is highly rated by both staff and students. It is, however, unclear how this service will operate in the future and much will depend on the terms of the UK digitisation licence that is currently being negotiated between the universities and the CLA. What is clear is that the ability to include full-text readings in online courses is attractive both to staff and students but is a complex service that needs adequate resources and staff to function effectively.

Case study 2: Online resource lists at the University of Sheffield

This second case study comes from the University of Sheffield Library and examines the introduction of an online reading list (or resource list) management system, which is integrated with the virtual learning environment. Sheffield has launched a number of projects to integrate library resources and e-learning initiatives and these are also briefly examined. Resource list management systems are a relatively new development, but there has been considerable interest in them in the UK recently. This is discussed in Chapter 1 in more detail. Two commercial systems exist: Sentient Discover[2] (formerly Reading Lists Direct) and TalisList, an independent module for the Talis Library Management System, which is also available separately as an integral unit in its own right.[3]

At Sheffield, the Library started to explore the feasibility of introducing such a system in 2001 and they chose TalisList for a number of reasons. TalisList is an additional module of the Talis Library Management System which is used at Sheffield, but additionally TalisList has the ability to link with WebCT, which is the institutional VLE. This means that a reading list can be 'plugged in' to a WebCT course so that changes made in the reading list are reflected in WebCT.

Introduction and background

The University of Sheffield was founded in 1905 and is part of the Russell Group, which are established research-led universities in the UK. Teaching covers a broad range of subjects and the University has seven faculties, including: Architectural Studies, Arts, Engineering, Law, Medicine, Pure Science and Social Sciences. As of 2003 there are over 23,000 students, from over 120 countries, and approximately 5,500 members of staff. The University's mission is to teach students in a research-led environment. Almost half the students are using the VLE WebCT and Sheffield is delivering 'blended learning' so that campus-based students can access course resources to support their face-to-face teaching. As of September 2003 there were just over 200 modules available online. The project is directly in line with the Library's Strategic Plan for 2003–06, which is looking to improve book availability for students through initiatives such as coursepacks and electronic off-prints.[4] The Strategic Plan also emphasises the need to build a 'new partnership with academic staff' to improve procedures for acquiring new learning resources.

Library projects in the VLE

There have been a number of library projects at Sheffield that seek to integrate electronic resources into the VLE. The focus of this case study is the introduction of online reading lists. However, this is one of a number of library initiatives which include:

- the development and roll-out of online reading lists with full-text links using the reading list management system TalisList, including their integration into WebCT;
- an electronic offprint (electronic coursepack) pilot service;
- access to electronic resources through the university portal, Muse;
- updating web pages and subject guides to fit the new content management system;
- online information skills tutorials to be delivered within WebCT.

The LibCT project

In the UK higher education community there has been considerable interest in resource list management systems. The interest was partly driven by the publication of a report from the DELIVER Project, comparing two commercial systems with an open source solution (Harris, 2003b). A number of universities decided to purchase a resource list management system following this report. However, the reading list project at Sheffield University was launched back in 2001. The University of Sheffield was already using Talis for its library management, therefore they chose to investigate and subsequently purchase the TalisList product soon after its launch. The project began in Autumn 2001 and was known as LibCT (Stubley, 2002a, 2002b). It was funded by the University of Sheffield Learning and Teaching Development Fund, and sought to explore the feasibility of integrating reading lists into WebCT, through the use of TalisList.

TalisList, like other resource list systems, enables links to be provided not just to printed material in the Library catalogue, but also to websites, full-text articles, chapters from e-books, handouts or PowerPoint slides created by the lecturer. This material is coordinated in a structured way. The system includes the facility to prioritise items, include annotations and organise the reading list to match the course format (e.g. by relevance of text, by week or seminar). The term 'resource list' is often used in place of reading list, as it represents a move away from a traditional paper reading list that contains books in the library, to an integrated approach to providing access to learning resources in whatever format.

User needs

Before launching the system, the team conducted research using in-depth interviews with a group of teaching staff who had experience of using WebCT. The research explored how the traditional concept of a reading list had altered in the online environment. It found that teaching staff wanted resources to be made available in a way that enabled students to work equally effectively in both the electronic and the traditional library environment. The tutors were also keen that the library should provide as many electronic readings as possible. The research raised a number of practical issues, including the need by lecturers to update a reading list to reflect any last-minute changes. This contrasts with the library's request for lists to be submitted at least three months before the start of the course to cope with ordering and processing new material, in addition to the substantial workloads associated with processing the reading lists.

Resource implications and staffing issues

At Sheffield, as with many other universities, it was agreed that library staff would set up the online reading lists, which has obvious resource implications. The intention was that once lists had been set up they could be edited by academic staff to take account of any changes. In the Main Library the Resources Team undertake a range of tasks including checking reading lists and preparing paper coursepacks. This group of staff were trained to use TalisList and add lists to the system. In the past, academic staff submitted their reading lists to the library to ensure materials were available for the start of teaching. Lists were usually received in Word format and could be checked to ensure the material was available. However, using TalisList an online list is created with links to the full-text resource where available. Links to electronic journals, web-based resources and any other electronic materials can therefore be inserted so that the student can access the full text.

At the various site libraries in Sheffield, reading lists were added to the TalisList system by staff based there. Therefore overall the creation of online reading lists was shared out among a number of library staff. In 2004 there were almost 2,000 lists available and 75 per cent of these lists include links to full-text articles in electronic journals.

Related developments

A related project is investigating the issues involved in establishing and managing an e-offprint service. Part of the work is to compare the costs and benefits of using the HERON Service versus in-house copyright clearance and digitisation. However, the project is also investigating the integration of the e-offprint service with the provision of online reading lists via TalisList. The project will evaluate the usage by students and academic staff and their preference for print coursepacks versus electronic packs, and estimate the resource requirements for rolling out the service more widely.

The roll out of the reading list system has also led to interesting discussions between library and academic staff about the nature and purpose of reading lists. Some staff were concerned that by providing links to full-text articles, students were being 'spoon-fed' while others saw this as essential 'scaffolding' to their learning. To counteract any claims of spoon-feeding, tutors are able to decided themselves whether a link directs a student straight to an article. The resource lists can also be used to integrate information skills into the curriculum. Parker (2004a) gives an excellent example of how this is happening:

> For example, in one of the nursing lists students are required to search for illustrations of the Ebola virus, and through annotation the Library staff have suggested how to carry out not only an image search but also how to search for phrases on Google.

Issues and concerns

Since the launch of TalisList a number of issues and concerns have been highlighted. Keeping lists up to date is proving problematic as TalisList currently does not have a link checker. This request has been passed to Talis. It is also a challenge to take a holistic approach to lists and coordinate between whether articles are available full text, as electronic offprints, included in printed coursepacks or as printed short loan offprints. For this reason Sheffield have purchased the Packtracker system[5] from HERON to try to manage this. The Library has found that since launching the project the problem of obtaining reading lists from academics in time to process them has not gone away. That said, academic staff have been impressed with the online system so the Library is receiving a higher percentage of lists than previously. At the time of writing this case study, the Library was just starting to revise old reading lists and believed it would be important to assess how much work is involved in editing existing lists as opposed to inputting from scratch.

Feedback and evaluation

Evaluation work was still ongoing at Sheffield at the time of writing, but work was being undertaken to examine the impact of the project on student satisfaction levels. Four modules for which the Library had provided digitised offprints were evaluated. The results found that there were no complaints about book availability and students in general regarded the provision as good – with those ranking the system as 'excellent' outweighing those saying 'fair'. They had very few problems with access and the only comments were about printers not working. They nearly all preferred electronic offprints to short loan but were divided equally between electronic coursepacks and printed coursepacks.

Feedback was also gathered from the lecturers who had been involved in the project. They were all enthusiastic and the Law and Psychology Departments noted an increase in citations within assignments and a general improvement in work. The final (internal) report will be available to inform future policy.

Conclusions and future developments

The work at Sheffield is ongoing and over the academic year (2004/5) the Library plan to offer training on TalisList for academic staff. This will mean that staff are able to edit their own reading lists on the system. Overall this initiative has been successful and the Library believes that through online reading lists they now have a real presence in the virtual learning environment.

Case study 3: The DELIVER project 'Library area'

The DELIVER project was part of the JISC-funded Digital Libraries and Virtual Learning Environments (DiVLE) Programme discussed in some detail in Chapter 2. There was considerable publicity generated by the project as it evaluated three reading list management systems. However, arguably a more important aspect of the project was the development of a model of how library resources could be integrated into the VLE using a 'Library area'. This model is now being used by many WebCT courses at the LSE and it forms part of the WebCT course template. The case study demonstrates a practical way in which different types of library resources can be integrated into the virtual learning environment.

Background and introduction

The DELIVER Project ran from October 2002 to June 2003 and was jointly led by the LSE and De Montfort University. It examined digital library and VLE integration by investigating three areas, including the development of:

- a generic library area within the VLE;
- subject-specific resource areas within the VLE;
- course-specific resource areas within the VLE.[6]

While much of the publicity focused on the evaluation of three reading list management systems, the project also undertook an extensive analysis of users' needs , focusing on academic staff and course designers at both institutions (Harris, 2003a). One of the recommendations to come out of this research was the need to establish a library area within the VLE. The report argued (p. 10) that this should include the following sections:

- information skills and student training;
- journal reading room for access to course supporting journal titles;
- multimedia resources;
- resource lists.

This recommendation was passed to the Centre for Learning Technology at the LSE for development work. Some experimentation was carried out using the tools already available in WebCT. The development also took place at the same time that the LSE were revising the icons used in WebCT. Therefore it was possible to design new icons to represent both the Library area and the specific tools that it contained.

The Library area

The first stage involved deciding where to place the Library area. Within WebCT and other VLEs there are numerous places that 'bookmarks' or links can be placed. Many institutions have a generic link to the library website within the VLE. However, as there were numerous tools and customisable links that the team wanted to add, it was decided that the Library area should be created from what WebCT calls an 'organiser page'. This is an icon which appears on the course home page and contains further links to other tools within it. An icon very much representative of the LSE Library was designed and within this organiser page were added links to numerous library-related tools and resources. Figure 6.4 shows the Library area icon within a WebCT course.

Figure 6.4 Screen shot of Library area in WebCT

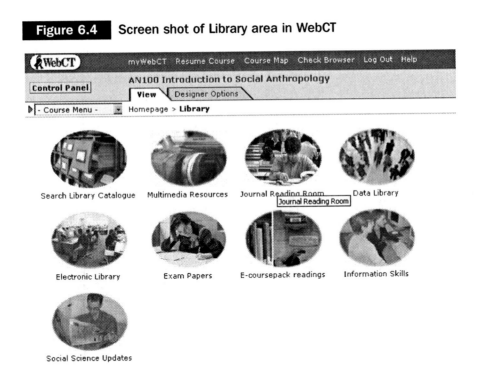

The tools in the Library area included generic resources, such as the library catalogue, but also other links that could be customised so that they are course specific. They included:

- a generic link to the Library Catalogue which can be searched from within WebCT – it was felt that a quick link to get to the library catalogue would be useful for all courses;

- a generic link to the Electronic Library, which is a database containing all the electronic resources at the LSE – this link could be customised to link to specific resources or to the relevant subject listing of resources;

- a generic link to the electronic journals listing, known as the Journal Reading Room – the LSE maintains a database of electronic journals and the link could be customised to link to specific titles or to the relevant subject listing of e-journals;

- a generic link to the exam paper database, which can be customised to link to the specific exam papers relevant for the course;

- a link to the information skills website, which has information about face-to-face classes and online courses;

- a link to the online reading list, where links to electronic coursepacks and e-journal articles are added into the online reading list template described in Case Study 2;

- a link to a page of RSS feeds from the SOSIG (SOcial Science Information Gateway) website that could be customised to include subject-specific resources.

The use of the Library area

The Library area was added to all new WebCT courses in 2003 as part of the standard template. Its use was promoted by the CLT staff in the course of WebCT training and support. Academic staff were able to hide any tools they did not want to use and customise the Library area to link to appropriate resources for their course. For example, one law course made significant use of a tool which enabled 'deep linking' at article level to resources held in the Westlaw database. These links were made available through an online reading list.

Problems and issues

One of the major problems associated with launching the Library area was how to promote it to academic staff. Many staff had already established means of providing links to resources integrated within their

WebCT course. They were reluctant to undertake major changes to their course. It was agreed that liaison librarians would be invited to become involved in populating the Library area to illustrate how it might be used. The Anthropology Department was chosen as a pilot for this work and the project is currently in progress to build a customised Anthropology Library Area.

New courses were provided with a WebCT course template, so it was relatively straightforward to incorporate the Library area into this template. Nevertheless, training and support for the effective use of the Library area was problematic. Simply making the Library area available in the WebCT template did not encourage its use, as staff required guidance. With only one librarian within the team, one-to-one support was not practical for a large number of academic staff. However, the team was fortunate in having the experience and skills of an IT trainer who, throughout 2003/04, worked with the librarian to develop training materials, including support documentation and a course handbook that could be used in group training sessions. The group training and support was being piloted with a small number of academics during the summer of 2004 with the plan being to launch the courses formally in the autumn as part of the Academic Staff Development Programme.

Evaluation and conclusion

Creating a Library area was a relatively straightforward task to undertake; however, to date, its use by academic staff in online courses at the LSE has been minimal. The support and training required to set up and build a customised Library area was significant. More formal training will commence in October 2004 and it is hoped that the library area will develop to a greater extent after this date.

Case study 4: Information literacy and the VLE at Imperial College, London

This final case study describes the development of an information literacy course delivered via the VLE at Imperial College, London.[7] Chapter 3 described how information literacy education (or information skills) is one of the most important areas in which librarians can become involved in e-learning initiatives. Many libraries have seen the VLE as a valuable vehicle for information literacy teaching, either by establishing separate online courses or by preparing materials that can be embedded into other courses. This case study shows how information literacy education can be delivered using a VLE and embedded into the curriculum. By using e-learning, students are able to study at a time and place convenient to them. All too often students complain that library induction, database classes and other information literacy skills are delivered at the wrong time in the wrong way. This case study shows that by using the VLE to deliver this type of education, many of these problems will be resolved.

Introduction and background

The Imperial College of Science, Technology and Medicine was established in 1907 as an independent constituent part of the University of London.[8] It is based in London's scientific and cultural heart, South Kensington, and was formed from the merger of the Royal College of Science, the City and Guilds College and the Royal School of Mines. Many famous scientists and engineers are associated with the College such as Sir Alexander Fleming and Sir Ernst Chain, discoverers of penicillin. The College has merged with numerous medical and scientific institutions and has campuses as far away as Wye College, based in Kent.

Imperial College's mission is to deliver

> ... world class scholarship, education and research in science, engineering and medicine, with particular regard to their application in industry, commerce and healthcare.[8]

The College has five faculties, including Engineering, Life Sciences, Humanities and Business, Medicine and Physical Sciences. In 2003 the College had approximately 10,000 full-time students, three-quarters of whom were undergraduates. Approximately 20 per cent of students come from outside the UK or EU and 70 per cent of the student body are men. Imperial College London Library consists of a central library largely responsible for supporting undergraduates. There are also eight departmental research libraries on the South Kensington campus and seven other campus libraries. In 2003 Imperial adopted WebCT as their institutional VLE and since this date library staff have been keen to investigate ways in which library resources can be integrated.

The incorporation of an online course into subject teaching

The case study is based on work undertaken through a collaboration of librarians, academics and information technologists from Imperial College, London. They developed an information literacy course for undergraduate engineering students using WebCT, known as Olivia – the OnLine virtual information assistant (see Figure 6.5).[9] The project started in April 2003 when an academic approached the Library with a proposal for an information literacy course for first-year undergraduate students in engineering. Discussions with the course manager started in July 2003, who wanted the course to be a blend of lectures, group work and 'hands on'. The decision was made to use WebCT to support the programme as it could be used to enhance classroom teaching as well as by students independently through self-paced learning. The programme was never seen as a replacement for teaching face-to-face classes. Moreover, the WebCT course was not designed to be an 'add on' to the course, but to be incorporated into the subject teaching. The development team worked to a tight deadline as the project needed to be completed by October 2003.

At the same time, library staff at Imperial had started work on an information literacy strategy, which they wanted to be cohesive and integrated into the curriculum. The staff used work such as the SCONUL

Figure 6.5 Opening screen of Olivia: OnLine virtual information assistant

seven pillars, the Australian and American standards and the results from the Big Blue Project (discussed in more detail in Chapter 3). The group were seeking a pedagogically sound, linear, information literacy teaching programme, delivered by competent information professionals which is assessed, embedded in the curriculum and consistently delivered throughout the college.

Staff implications and resources

The decision to launch an online course had staff development issues. Consequently, in preparation for the development of the course, the staff involved in the project attended a training course on pedagogy and e-learning. They experienced a steep learning curve, not just learning the technical skills they required to build the course in WebCT, but in learning how to design and teach online courses. They found that they couldn't simply upload their existing resources into WebCT, but needed to rethink the entire programme and make it suitable for delivery using 'blended learning'.

Technical issues

WebCT includes numerous tools to facilitate online learning, including discussion tools, assessment tools, and a Content Module, whereby course materials can be uploaded. The Library decided to use the quiz tool in WebCT to create a pre-course questionnaire to identify the students' skills levels and the resources they were accustomed to using. In addition to using the WebCT tools, the Library used a number of other pieces of software to build the course components. The content of the course mainly existed in Microsoft Word format. Therefore, to speed up the development process, the Library decided to use the CourseGenie software.[10] This allows course materials prepared in Microsoft Word format to be converted and uploaded into WebCT very quickly.

On reflection, although this meant the information was uploaded quickly, the team found the software inflexible and the design was therefore restricted. In addition to written course notes, Microsoft PowerPoint presentations featured in the course. Library staff used a product known as Impatica[11] to shrink the size of these PowerPoint presentations so they would run faster and use less space. Finally, in any information literacy course it can be necessary to demonstrate what is occurring on the screen. In a face-to-face class this can be done using a projector to allow students to see the steps they need to take, e.g. when accessing an online database and undertaking a search. However, software is also available to provide animated online demonstrations. Imperial decided to use the Viewlets software to create a number of online demonstrations.[12] Although this was successful, future developments will include interactive tutorials produced using software from the INHALE project.[13]

Programme contents

Students can use the Olivia programme either remotely or in the classroom. It contains seven self-contained units that can be used either selectively or as a linear programme. The topics covered are:

- an introduction to info-literacy;
- searching and retrieving skills;
- Internet skills;
- databases;
- critical evaluation;
- acquiring and managing your references;
- referencing.

Goals were laid out at the start of each unit, including aims and learning outcomes. At the end of each unit there was assessment in the form of a multiple-choice self-test. This enabled students to check their own progress using this feature. As the results are not recorded, students found this feature useful to test their personal development. The course was subject-specific for engineering students (see Figure 6.6), with specific examples of searches in databases relevant to this group. However, the materials were developed so they could be reused and adapted for other subjects.

Student feedback and evaluation

Feedback and evaluation from students on the course was extremely positive. The library staff found that students took the course very seriously; this was partly attributed to the use of online assessment and the fact that it was embedded in the subject teaching. In particular, new international students, who were still unsure of English, found the course useful as it allowed them to go through the material several times and

Figure 6.6 A screenshot of Olivia delivered by Imperial's VLE: WebCT

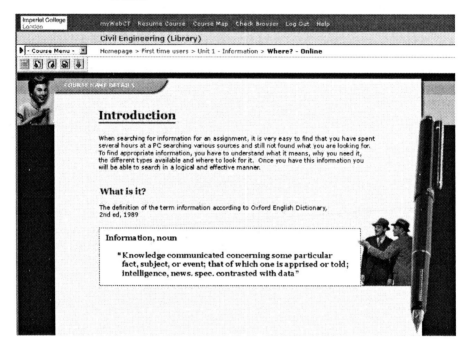

then test themselves. Students also requested that they be allowed to access the course beyond the first year, because it was so useful. Many reported that after taking the course they realised what information literacy was and how important and useful the skills were. The course was rolled out throughout the academic year and student feedback showed that they wanted some units earlier as they proved so useful in other courses.

Problems and concerns

Overall, the project had relatively few problems, although the staff did acknowledge that there was a steep learning curve in the development process. The Library also concluded that it found the CourseGenie software problematic and decided that in future it would prepare materials in HTML from scratch as this was easier. It also found that the Viewlets were restrictive, and was looking at using a different type of software to record from the screen.

Future developments

The development of Olivia at Imperial has been heralded as a success and library staff are planning a number of developments for the next academic year. For example, it has been agreed that the discussion tool will be used in the course for the next year. The Library is also planning to expand the referencing unit to become a Plagiarism and Referencing Module. The materials developed in Olivia were intended to be customisable for other subject disciplines and a course for agricultural and biological sciences is planned next.

More significantly, the course has been awarded an internal Teaching and Learning Grant to develop more online courses. These grants are usually given out to academic departments at Imperial and this is the first time the Library has been awarded a teaching grant. Staff are extremely pleased as this is excellent for raising the profile of the Library and demonstrating that it makes a valuable contribution to teaching.

Using electronic journal resources: a practical guide

Electronic journals are perhaps one of the easiest and most valuable library resources that can be integrated into a virtual learning environment. In higher education, the vast majority of academic disciplines rely on journals as a means of scholarly communication and students at both undergraduate and postgraduate levels need access to this material. In many instances teaching staff have designated readings, i.e. lists they expect students to complete, perhaps before attending a class or seminar. At the same time, many academic libraries now have a growing collection of electronic journals, for which they pay increasingly large subscriptions. It is therefore imperative that the library fully exploits these resources. Consequently, linking to journal resources from the VLE makes sense for both teachers and librarians. Licences rather than copyright law governs the use of e-journals, therefore in all instances librarians should check carefully the specific terms and conditions that govern use at their institution. However, electronic journal providers are increasingly realising the value of allowing their content to be used in this way and make provision for this both legally in the licensing agreement and practically by providing linking advice.

This section is a practical guide to using electronic journal resources, based on the instructions developed at the London School of Economics and Political Science for creating links to widely used e-journal aggregator services. While the range of titles and list of providers will vary across institutions, as we have seen in Chapter 5, the concept of linking is becoming increasingly standardised, using OpenURL and the Digital Object Identifier (DOI). The guide is aimed at librarians, to serve as a basis for designing their own e-journal linking guide. It may also be of value to course designers or academic staff; however, the full listing of electronic journals available at your institution will need to be investigated. The stable links can then be pasted into online reading lists of some form. More information about online reading lists is available in Case study 2.

General principles when linking

When linking to electronic journals at article level it is important to use a 'stable URL', i.e. a link that will remain constant throughout commercial or archival changes (such as a change of publisher). Some electronic journals allow you to create stable links to an article simply by using the URL or web address you get when you retrieve the article. In other databases, for example JSTOR and Ingenta, URLs contain session information that will expire after a period of time so cannot be used to create stable links. Therefore they cannot by copied and used in online bibliographies or course websites. These databases often provide a method for generating stable URLs which can then be used to create article-level links. You should also note:

- there may be authentication problems linking to some databases, which means users are prompted for a password;
- some of the electronic journals may not be accessible from outside your institutional network because of the licence agreement and the use of IP authentication. This means that links will only work within your network and users will need to be notified.

Locating electronic journal titles

The first phase in creating links to e-journals is ensuring that academics are easily able to identify the range of titles to which your institution subscribes. This is often not as easy as you might think, particularly when titles are purchased from a number of aggregators. Increasingly, academic libraries are purchasing serials management systems, such as

TDNet and Serials Solutions, to solve this problem and ensure their users have an up-to-date list of e-journal titles. However, many institutions maintain separate listings of e-journals or use the library catalogue. Whatever method is used, do consider that to fully exploit the range of titles to which you are subscribing, users must be able to easily identify the titles they need.

Creating stable URLs

To create stable URLs there are two approaches:

- using DOIs;
- creating stable URLs directly.

Using DOIs (Digital Object Identifiers)

DOIs are discussed in some detail in Chapter 5. They are unique, unchanging numbers or 'global identifiers', designed to facilitate the location and management of digital objects or content, such as electronic journal articles. More than merely 'links' they are unique identifiers that allow global access to the content as long as you are entitled to that content through an institutional subscription.

What do they look like and where do I find them?

DOIs are typically found on the top left-hand corner of abstracts, mentioned in the Table of Contents, printed at the top or bottom of an article, alongside traditional citation details and in bibliographic lists. They typically appear thus:

> DOI: 10.1239/jap/1019737983

DOIs are composed of a prefix and a suffix. The prefix always begins with 10.xxxx/ where xxxx is a unique number assigned to a registrant in the DOI system (usually a publisher). For example, 10.1016 refers to Elsevier. The suffix specifies an individual item/document.

How do I use DOIs?

To use DOIs in web browsers it is necessary to prefix the DOI with the URL of a DOI resolver. Therefore all DOIs must be prefixed by:

> *http://dx.doi.org/*

Make sure you don't leave any spaces when copying and pasting DOIs as these will be interpreted as part of the number and the item will not be resolved correctly.

What should I do if I have any problems?

You can still continue to create stable links to journal articles using the methods described below. Both methods will work independently of each other.

Which e-journals use DOIs and which do not?

An increasing number of electronic journals are using DOIs, including titles available on Swetswise, Ingenta and Science Direct. However, it depends on the journal publisher not just the e-journal provider, so you will need to check for each journal article you wish to link to.

Titles available through the following services do not include DOIs, so please consult the information about creating stable links to these titles:

- JSTOR;
- Westlaw.

Can I retrieve a DOI using a journal reference?

DOIs can be retrieved from CrossRef's DOI lookup system, which permits registered libraries to submit batch requests. Individual requests can also be submitted using CrossRef's web form (*http://www.crossref .org/02publishers/37guest_query.html*). In order to retrieve a DOI you will need to supply the journal title, author's name or start page of the article. CrossRef recommend using the journal title instead of the ISSN. A list of journal titles in the CrossRef holdings is available in a browsable format on the web page. By entering the bibliographic details into the web form you can retrieve a DOI for the articles. The interface is not intended for automated querying and if you need to query CrossRef on an automated batch basis, you will need to obtain an account on the system. There is no charge for libraries to set up a CrossRef account to retrieve DOIs or metadata. For more information see the CrossRef Libraries web page (*http://www.crossref.org/03libraries/index.html*).

Linking to e-journal examples

The method for linking to electronic journals depends on which aggregator or publisher delivers it, although many are now using OpenURL or DOIs. Several libraries maintain up-to-date listings of the linking method used by a range of electronic journal providers, for example the listing by the London School of Economics.[14] Below is a selection of examples from some of the major electronic journal services.

Electronic collections online provided by OCLC FirstSearch

Electronic Collections Online (ECO) offers web access to an increasing range of electronic journals from over 70 publishers. Access to the titles is via OCLC's FirstSearch (*http://www.oclc.org/firstsearch/*) which links through to full-text articles, where these are available. Linking to journal title, journal table of contents and also article level is possible through this service. However, note that these instructions will work only if you are viewing a page that has full text. Also note that the links will only work within your institutional network as they are IP authenticated. To link to an article:

1. View the full text of desired article.
2. Click link pickup icon located in the top right-hand corner of the screen.
3. Select and copy the URL that appears below the text 'IP-address recognition URL for direct article access'.
4. Paste as needed into your course website or online bibliography.

More help and support with 'Direct Article Access' is available from the OCLC website (*http://www.oclc.org/*).

Ingenta journals

Ingenta (*http://www.ingenta.com*) has an ever-growing collection of journal material, including over 16 million articles from more than 28,000 titles. Your institution is likely to subscribe to a proportion of these titles and numerous deals are available. It is possible to link to journal titles and articles on Ingenta using the OpenURL standard to generate a stable URL. Authorised use of Ingenta includes:

- bookmarking an article to e-mail the URL to colleagues;

- making specific articles available to users from your website;
- creating a direct link to a publication.

To create a link to a publication, you can use Ingenta EasyLink bookmarks, or copy and paste the title of the publication from the list of title URLs. To create a direct link to an article note:

- Ingenta uses the OpenURL standard for linking to articles. These URLs are based on the OpenURL standard and will not change;
- an OpenURL takes the following form:

http://openurl.ingenta.com/content?genre=article ....

To create a link to a specific article, the URL must contain the following fields:

ISSN (international standard serial number)

Volume

Issue

Page number of first page of the article (spage)

An article can be therefore be specified by its bibliographic data, as follows:

Issn=0960-2585

Volume=9

Issue=2

Spage=111

The OpenURL uses a standard formula and the link to the above publication will look as follows:

http://openurl.ingenta.com/content?genre=article&issn=0960-2585&volume=9&issue=2&spage=111

Detailed information is available from the Ingenta website and your representative can also advise further about this method.

JSTOR

JSTOR (*http://www.jstor.org/*) has numerous electronic journal collections available including titles in the Arts and Sciences. All articles available from JSTOR provide full text. Stable URLs, which differ from the URLs that display when you are viewing an article, are available for all articles. They are provided on search results screens, tables of contents screens and citation screens. Or you can obtain a stable URL when you are viewing an article by following the steps below:

1. View any page of the full text of the desired article.
2. Click on the citation/stable URL link near the top or the bottom of the page.
3. Select the URL and copy and paste as needed.
4. Optional – at the end of the URL you add 'origin=YOUR INSTITUTION' (for example 'origin=LSE' for the London School of Economics). This provides an identifier for JSTOR staff, which they use if they need to locate problematic links. It shouldn't affect the way the links work.

JSTOR has adopted the Serial Item and Contribution Identifier (SICI) standard as an article-level identifier. SICI is an ANSI/NISO standard that was developed to uniquely identify serial items, typically issues, and their contributions, typically articles. This is discussed in more detail in Chapter 5.

JSTOR has also developed the Citation Linking Tool to automate the creation of stable URLs based on the citation information you submit via an online form. The resultant URLs may be cut and pasted into your web-based teaching materials

Swetswise

Swetswise (*https://www.swetswise.com/*) is another large e-journal aggregator, with over 8,000 titles available from more than 300 publishers. Swetswise use a multi-level linking algorithm based on OpenURL to generate stable links to their material. Similar to Ingenta, URLs are defined by ISSN, volume, issue and page number. The authentication of requests for articles is currently done by IP recognition, although the journals can be accessed using an Athens authentication. However, links to journal or article level will only work on your institutional network.

Linking typically uses title information and can be done at three different levels:

1. Journal level – only the journal name is linked to and Swetswise will reveal the list of issues available with links to TOCs, abstract and full text.
2. Issue level – available issues can be linked to and Swetswise will reveal the TOC with links to abstract and full text.
3. Article level – here Swetswise would link directly to the article's abstract or the full text.

The URL structure is as follows:

> *http://www.swetswise.com/link/access_db?issn=&vol=&iss=&part= &page=&year=*

In the example above, the following tags should be completed with the following bibliographic details:

Issn=ISSN number (with or without hyphen)

Vol=Volume number

Iss=Issue number

Part=Part type – e.g. 'SUPPL' in case of supplement (optional)

Page=start page number

Year=Publication year

To link directly into the full text of an article, add &FT=1 to the string. For example, to link to the journal article:

RICARDO GOMEZ and JOHN PETERSON. The EU's Impossibly Busy Foreign Ministers: 'no one is in control', *European Foreign Affairs Review*, 6: 53–74, 2001

you would use the URL:

> *http://www.swetswise.com/link/access_db?issn=13846299&vol=6& iss=1&page=53&year=2001*

Some publishers available through Swetswise do not allow access directly to full text, however, and for those publishers you will access an abstract page which easily navigates users to the full text.

Westlaw

Westlaw (*http://www.westlaw.com/*) is a major source of electronic journal information and other legal material, including legislation and law reports. However, linking to journal titles and articles is possible: you will need to contact your Westlaw representative for more information. Westlaw have created an article linking tool, which generates a stable URL from the legal citation. This tool is highly valuable and enables academic staff to create deep links into Westlaw so that students can easily find the material they need.

Science Direct

Science Direct (*http://www.www.sciencedirect.com/*) is one of the largest collections of science, technology and medical information, containing the Elsevier journal titles with almost 6 million full-text articles. Science Direct are using Digital Object Identifiers (DOIs) for all their journal articles to allow users to create stable links. The method for linking is very straightforward:

1. Locate the journal article you wish to link to.
2. From the table of contents click on the 'SummaryPlus' link.
3. At the top of the page the DOI is available, which will take the following format:

   Doi:10.1016/s0038-1101(03)00101-1 Cite or link using doi

4. Right click on the link above and 'Copy Shortcut'. You will now have a stable link to the article which can be pasted into a reading list.

For more information about DOIs see the Science Direct website.

EBSCO

EBSCO (*http://www.www.ebsco.com/home/*) is an important electronic journal provider in the field of business studies. It is very easy to link to full-text articles available on EBSCO. Do not copy the link from the browser window. Instead, when viewing the citation of an article that you wish to link to, copy the URL from the field labelled 'Persistent Link to this Article'. A typical persistent or stable URL will look as follows:

http://search.epnet.com/direct.asp?An=11502173&db=buh

MetaPress

MetaPress (*http://www.metapress.com/*) is an example of a smaller e-journal provider that is also supporting the OpenURL standard. Using this provider, it is possible to link at journal, issue and article level to these titles. To locate the stable URL of either a journal title, issue or article, use the 'Linking Options' link which is displayed in the citation information. You can use the MetaPress Direct Linking method – simply copy and paste the URL into your reading list. Alternatively MetaPress provide an Open URL which can be copied and pasted into your reading list.

For example, to link directly to an article in Volume 46, Number 5/2003 of the *Academy of Management Journal*, you may use:

- MetaPress Direct Linking:

  http://www.metapress.com/link.asp?id=wp089dr8djh0vgbn or

- OpenURL:

  http://www.metapress.com/openurl.asp?genre=article&issn=0001-4273&volume=46&issue=5&spage=539

Linking to other e-journal resources

Numerous other electronic journals are available and it is not possible to include detailed linking instructions for all these resources. However, many use the same formula or methods described above. In the first instance, the Serials Team in your library should be able to provide you with contacts at the different companies, who are usually excellent sources of information. They can advise you about whether linking to resources in this way is covered by your licence, any tools that have been set up to facilitate linking the standards that are being adhered to, as well as offering general advice and support. If linking in this way is not available, your inquiry may well lead to the development of this service and they should be able to offer an alternative solution, such as allowing articles to be downloaded and used in the VLE, under the terms of your licence.

Care has been taken to ensure the instructions are as up to date as possible. However, this area is one in which developments take place rapidly, therefore it is recommended you contact either your representative at the various companies or their website for more information.

Conclusion

This final chapter has highlighted a number of different approaches to integrating library resources with virtual learning environments. The case studies highlight that there are a number of ways in which librarians can become involved in e-learning initiatives as UK academic libraries are developing new services. The electronic environment has provided libraries with an opportunity to exploit and extend their role in learning. The key to that success is integration of systems, but also collaboration and joint projects with both technologists but also educators.

Notes

1. See: *http://heronweb.ingenta.com/packtrackerdemo/*
2. See: *http://www.sentientlearning.com/home*
3. See: *http://www.talis.com/*
4. University of Sheffield Library Strategic Plan 2003–06 (2004). Available from: *http://www.shef.ac.uk/library/libdocs/strategicplan0306.pdf*
5. See: *http://www.heron.ingenta.com/about/about_packtracker.html*
6. See: *http://www.angel.ac.uk/DELIVER/*
7. See: *http://www.imperial.ac.uk/*
8. See: *http://www.imperial.ac.uk/P2400.htm*
9. The Programme was previously known as OLIVE, but changed its name in 2004 to avoid confusion with another project of the same name.
10. See: *http://www.coursegenie.com/*
11. See: *http://www.impatica.com/*
12. See: *http://www.qarbon.com/products/viewlet/*
13. For more information see Chapter 3.
14. See: *http://teaching.lse.ac.uk/tech/ejournals.htm*

References

Boden, Debbi and Holloway, Sue (2004) *Virtually there: VLES and libraries: May 26th 2004*. A CPD25/UC&R London seminar. Olivia: OnLine virtual information assistant. Available from: *http://www .library.qmul.ac.uk/socsci/virtually%20there.htm*.

Harris, N. (2003a) *DELIVER. User Needs Analysis Report.* Available from: *http://www.angel.ac.uk/DELIVER/deliverables/UNA_final.doc.*

Harris, N. (2003b) *Resource list management systems: analysis of TalisList, ReadingList Direct, and Bookworm.* February 2003. Available from: *http://www.jisc.ac.uk/uploaded_documents/deliver_RLM_analysis.doc.*

Markland, M. (2003) 'Embedding online information resources in virtual learning environments: some implications for lecturers and librarians of the move towards delivering teaching in the online environment', *Information Research*, 8(4), paper 158. Available from: *http://informationr.net/ir/8-4/paper158.html.* Accessed 8 January 2004.

Parker, Lyn (2004a) *Blended learning, blended resources: a collaborative approach to supporting students*, paper presented at the Networked Learning Conference at Lancaster University, 5–7 April 2004. Available from: *http://www.shef.ac.uk/nlc2004/Proceedings/.*

Parker, Lyn (2004b) Rethinking reading lists: making effective use of online resource lists and electronic offprints to support students, *Assignation*, June.

Parker, Lyn (2004c) Rethinking reading lists. Presentation to the Assign AGM, 26 April 2004, at Aslib HQ. Available from: *http://www.lse.ac.uk/library/other_sites/aliss/parker.ppt.*

Stubley, P. (2002a) 'Going beyond resource discovery', *Library and Information Update*, 1(7): 34–5.

Stubley, P. (2002b) 'Skills move to VLEs', *Library and Information Update*, 1(6): 52–4.

7

Conclusion

E-learning has arisen from the information and communication technological revolution and, like other forms of technology, it is undoubtedly facilitating change across the education sector. Libraries have always been an integral part of learning, helping learners find, evaluate and exploit resources. Therefore it is unsurprising that changes in education are being felt in the library profession. With an increasing number of digital resources, librarians have a crucial role in navigating learners through the complex digital information environment. They also have an important role advising staff about copyright and licensing issues associated with e-learning. Furthermore, library systems need to be integrated with e-learning systems and interoperability is the key to future success. If librarians are not involved in e-learning initiatives there is a real danger that learners might bypass the library altogether.

If you have read this far then I would hope that you want to take action and get involved in e-learning initiatives, and I would hope you now understand why you need to do this. E-learning is not something that is happening outside of the library. E-learning should also not be regarded as a threat to libraries and librarians. E-learning provides us with an opportunity. For too long librarians have sat on the sidelines rather than being regarded as equal partners to faculty members and educators. E-learning offers us an opportunity to redress this imbalance, to capitalise on our skills and expertise and to be recognised for our true value. Rather than repeat much of the arguments of previous chapters, this book ends with a ten-step plan for the librarian who wants to take action and who wants to move from the sidelines and work alongside educators.

Ten steps to getting into e-learning

- Get out of the library and network with educators, technologists and administrators. Go to conferences outside the library community and ensure that at every possible opportunity you are demonstrating the central role that you, as a librarian, play in the learning process.

- Seize opportunities to learn about learning and e-learning. Do a short course or spend time researching how to put a course online, to ensure any e-learning that you become involved in is well designed and pedagogically sound. Further reading is suggested in Chapter 2.

- Develop an information literacy programme that is integrated with the curriculum and uses innovative teaching methods as shown in the case study from Imperial College in Chapter 6. Work with learning technologists and educators to do this.

- The presentation of library resources in the VLE is currently a real issue. Consider establishing a 'library area' in your virtual learning environment with customised content as this will encourage teaching staff to think about library resources from the outset. See in particular the case study from the DELIVER Project in Chapter 6.

- There are many existing library resources that can be embedded into online courses at no extra cost. Ensure that you work with teaching staff who are building online courses to exploit library resources and embed these into the courses alongside Internet resources. Make sure that teaching staff are exploiting your subscriptions to electronic journals, electronic books and other resources.

- Online reading lists provide common ground between librarians and academic staff. They enable librarians to open up a dialogue with academic staff. The provision of reading lists within the VLE enhances the teaching support role of the library and is much appreciated by teaching staff.

- Get involved in staff development: information literacy for staff is just as important as for students. Don't assume that your staff know what information literacy is and why it is so important. More advice about this is available in Chapter 3.

- Learn about metadata standards and other specifications outlined in Chapter 5. This will help you when talking to learning technologists and other staff outside of the library.

- Consider setting up an e-print repository for staff publications if one does not already exist at your organisation. This is an area where librarians have been leading the way and can really help teaching staff.

- Investigate funding opportunities for library and e-learning projects in your organisation and then make sure you are driving these projects.

Appendix 1

Sample letter to the owner of a website to request permission to download material for educational use

Dear Sir/Madam

LSE Library and the Centre for Learning Technology wish to obtain your permission to include the following material in a secure course website for LSE staff and students. Rather than link to the material, we would like to download this article and make it available from our secure website. The material will be purely for educational purposes and will be delivered as part of an online course:

Richards, Claire. (2003, Friday, November 21) Mobilising the e-vangelists. *Guardian Unlimited*. Available at: http://education.guardian.co.uk/elearning/story/0,10577,1089683,00.html

The material will be used for the following course:

Course code and title:	**MC111 Media and communication**
Lecturer:	**Dr J Talgarth**
Student numbers:	**45**
Permission duration:	**October 2004 – July 2005**

The file will be stored on an LSE server and delivered as part of a WebCT course. Access will therefore be controlled by the use of password authentication and the file will NOT be available on the Internet.

What do you need to do?

To save time and trouble, a form is available [see below] which I would be grateful if you could complete and return to me. If you require payment, our preferred method of payment is a licence fee for the file.

If you have any questions, please do not hesitate to contact me.

Yours sincerely

Dr Jane Secker
Assistant Librarian (Learning Technology)

LSE Library/Centre for Learning Technology

Copyright declaration form

OUR REF: MC111/JS
DATE: 1/8/2004
REPLY NEEDED BY: 30/8/2004
PRODUCTION DATE: October 2004

Please reply to:
Centre for Learning Technology, LSE, Houghton Street, London, WC2A 2AE

Description of material
Richards, Claire. (2003, Friday, November 21) Mobilising the e-vangelists. *Guardian Unlimited.* Available at: http://education.guardian .co.uk/elearning/story/0,10577,1089683,00.html

Reproductions required for:

Course code and title:	**MC111 Media and communication**
Lecturer:	**Dr J Talgarth**
Student numbers:	**45**
Permission duration:	**October 2004 – July 2005**

I/We,

as owners of the reproduction rights, agree that **LONDON SCHOOL OF ECONOMICS AND POLITICAL SCIENCE, BLPES, 10 Portugal Street, London WC1A 2HD** may reproduce the material for the purposes stated. We require:

*No fee

*A fee of _____

(*Delete whichever is inappropriate.)

Dated:
Signed:

Appendix 2

Sample letter to a publisher to request permission to use an extract from a printed journal

Date

Dear Sir/Madam,

ELECTRONIC COPYRIGHT PERMISSION REQUEST

LSE Library and the Centre for Learning Technology wish to obtain your permission to convert the following material to digital format and make it available for a limited period, with appropriate security and access arrangements, to LSE staff and students. The reading is purely for educational purposes and will be delivered as part of an electronic course pack:

Extract details:

Author:	Weber, M
Title:	The definition of sociology and social action
Page range:	4-26

From source:

ISBN/ISSN:	0520028244
Author:	Weber, M
Title:	Economy and Society
Publication year:	1978

The reading has been designated as essential reading for the following course:

Course code and title:	**AN101 Ethnography and theory**
Lecturer:	**Dr M Madden**
Student numbers:	**46**
Permission duration:	**01/10/2004 to 01/09/2005**

The electronic copy of the article(s) will be made available in PDF format. We would also make back-up copies for security in the event of losing the master copy. The article will be stored on an LSE server and delivered as part of a WebCT course. Access will therefore be controlled by the use of password authentication. In compliance with the CLA Digitisation Licence full bibliographic details, a copyright statement and digitisation disclaimer will be appended to the front of each article.

What do you need to do?
To save time and trouble, a form is available [see below] which I would be grateful if you could complete and return to the Library. If you require payment, our preferred method of payment is a licence fee per article.

Yours faithfully

Dr Jane Secker
Assistant Librarian (Learning Technology)

LSE Library/Centre for Learning Technology

Copyright declaration form

Please return to:
Taught Course Support, LSE, Houghton Street, 10 Portugal Street, London, WC2A 2HD. United Kingdom.

Our ref:	**1514**
Date:	**12th September 2004**
Reply needed by:	**29/09/2004**
Production date:	**29/09/2004**

Description of material
Extract details:
Author: Weber, M
Title: The definition of sociology and social action
Page range: 4-26

From source:
ISBN/ISSN: 0520028244
Author: Weber, M
Title: Economy and Society
Publication year: 1978

Reproductions required for:
Course code and title: AN101 Ethnography and theory
Lecturer: Dr M Madden
Student numbers: 46
Permission duration: 01/10/2004 to 01/09/2005

I/We,
as owners of the reproduction rights, agree that LONDON SCHOOL OF ECONOMICS AND POLITICAL SCIENCE, BLPES, 10 Portugal Street, London WC1A 2HD may reproduce the material for the purposes stated. We require:

*No fee

*A fee of _____

(*Delete whichever is inappropriate.)

Dated:
Signed:

Glossary and commonly used abbreviations

New acronyms and terminology are emerging from the e-learning field all the time. There are a number of glossaries and encyclopedias available on the Web; below is a small selection which can be accessed for up-to-date terminology.

JISC Glossary: *http://www.jisc.ac.uk/index.cfm ?Name=about_glossary*
This glossary provides links to other areas of the JISC website, or to the websites of other organisations where appropriate. It is not specific to e-learning, but is a valuable resource to help understand acronyms and terms relating to technology and education.

CETIS reference: *http://www.cetis.ac.uk /encyclopedia*
A UK-based web resource aimed at the UK higher and further education community and providing definitions of the terms used in learning technology standards.

The Encyclopedia of Educational Technology: *http://coe.sdsu.edu/eet/*
Published by the Department of Educational Technology at San Diego State University. Articles are available on the topics of instructional design and education and training. It is aimed at those with minimal experience in the field.

E-learning Guru Glossary: *http://www.e-learningguru.com/gloss.htm*
Describes itself as the 'world's biggest, or at least most irreverent, e-Learning glossary!' Defines a variety of terms associated with e-learning and also includes a monthly newsletter you can subscribe to.

A small number of terms and acronyms and abbreviations associated with virtual learning environments and digital libraries are defined below.

ALT   Association of Learning Technologists – professional body to represent learning technologists

CETIS   Centre for Educational Technology Interoperability Standards

CMC   Computer Mediated Communication

DC   Dublin Core – metadata standard to describe library resources

DfES   Department for Education and Skills – UK government department responsible for education

DiVLE   Digital Library and Virtual Learning Environments – a JISC programme of research investigating integration between these two fields

DOI   Digital Object Identifier

HE   Higher education – the collective term for universities in the UK

ILTHE   Institute of Learning and Teaching in Higher Education, now being replaced by the Higher Education Academy

IMS   IMS Global Learning Consortium Ltd – responsible for specifications and standards in learning technology

JISC   Joint Information Systems Committee – funded by UK higher education funding councils

LOM   Learning Object Metadata – metadata used to describe 'learning objects', which are any digital resource used in learning, for example a piece of content, a self-test, a PowerPoint presentation, etc.

LMS   To a librarian this term means Library Management System, but beware, learning technologists may mean Learning Management System – or VLE – when they use this term

LTSN   Learning and Teaching Support Network

MLE   Managed Learning Environment

MCQs   Multiple Choice Questions – often used in online assessments

NSF   National Science Foundation

OAI   Open Archives Initiative

OSI   Open Source Initiative

PBL   Problem-Based Learning

SCORM   Shareable Courseware Object Reference Model

VLE   Virtual Learning Environment

Index

Printed in the United States
22798LVS00003B/253-324